Making Victorians

The Drummond Children's World

1827-1832

Making Victorians

The Drummond Children's World

1827-1832

by Susan Lasdun

Illustrated by the Drummond Children

LONDON
VICTOR GOLLANCZ LTD
1983

"To Priscil"

Copyright © Susan Lasdun 1983

The illustrations in this book are Crown copyright, reproduced by permission of the Victoria & Albert Museum.
Material from the Royal Archives is used by gracious permission of Her Majesty The Queen.

British Library Cataloguing in Publication Data
Lasdun, Susan
  Making Victorians
  1. Children — History — 19th century
  2. Great Britain — Social life and customs — 19th century
  I. Title   II. Drummond (*Family*)
  941.081   HQ792.G7

  ISBN 0-575-03176-X

Designed by Rupert Kirby

Printed in Italy by Sagdos S.p.A.
for Imago Publishing Limited

By the same author
Victorians at Home

ACKNOWLEDGEMENTS

Of the many printed sources to which I referred in my research there is one to which I am particularly indebted; this is Nancy Cutt's absorbing and scholarly study *Mrs Sherwood and Her Books for Children* (published 1974, OUP).

I am grateful to Anna Horovitz, Anthony Burton, Director of the Museum of Childhood, and his colleagues, Caroline Goodfellow and Noreen Marshall, for initially encouraging me and putting me on course with my research. I am also grateful to Anne Renier and Irene Whalley for suggesting further literary sources; and Pamela Davies and Dr Alfred White Franklin for their advice on paediatric ones.

I would like to thank Isobel Kenrick at the Royal Commission on Historic Manuscripts; Jane Langton, Registrar of the Royal Archives; Jessie Woodward of Rickmansworth Historical Society; and Clive Wainwright at the Victoria and Albert Museum, for their help.

I must thank, too, those people who so kindly sent me records of childhood in their possession: in particular Iris Fenton, who once more entrusted me with Fanny Drummond's album; Denys Tweddell, who translated and sent me the prescriptions for the Percy Family; Lady Elton, who sent drawings and essays from her family archives, and Lady Harrod for lending me the Memoir of the Reverend Gurney.

For their advice and expertise, I am extremely grateful to Mary Dunbar of the London Library, Ian Hessenberg who photographed the children's drawings, Mark Girouard who gave me the benefit of his scholarly comments, my son James who first read and corrected my manuscript, and for their typing, Christina Mill and Sally Newton.

Augusta, a diminutive member of the circle. Her puffed sleeves, décolletée neckline and nipped in waist emulates the dresses of her older siblings.

CONTENTS

Preface		14
1	THE FAMILY AND THEIR CIRCLE	15
2	NURSERY YEARS	25
3	THE SCHOOLROOM OR EDUCATION AT HOME	33
4	PUNISHMENT AND CORRECTION	43
5	LEISURE AND PLEASURE	51
6	FASHIONABLE ATTIRE	63
7	FAMILY RETAINERS	75
8	EPILOGUE	84
Notes		86
Index		93

PREFACE

THE HISTORY OF childhood is an elusive and fragmentary one, a reflection in part of the low esteem in which childhood was held. Generally regarded as an imperfect stage in the development of adulthood, to be hurried through as quickly as possible, its ephemeral nature was hardly deemed significant enough to record. Primary sources for it are rare and rarer still are those from children themselves. Therefore, the drawings by the Drummond children, crude and naïve though they are, give a unique glimpse into the world in which they lived and how they themselves perceived it. They are the inspiration for this book and the scenes and people they depict, together with the miscellaneous writings of their contemporary and cousin, Fanny Drummond, provide the topics. These sources enable us to elicit some of the current attitudes to childhood and, at the same time, give us a wealth of illuminating details, ranging from dress to servants. The book is essentially about childhood, and I have tried to show how these young contemporaries of Princess Victoria were moulded like her into the unmistakable members of the age to which she gave her name.

Susan Lasdun
London, April 1983

THE FAMILY
AND THEIR CIRCLE

THE DRUMMOND CIRCLE, as the drawings disclose, was peopled by those of rank and fortune, most of whom were related to one another and to the Drummond children. The children's father was Andrew Mortimer Drummond, a great-grandson of the founder of Drummonds Bank of Charing Cross and himself a partner in the same bank. Descended from an impeccable line of Scottish forebears, he joined his faultless lineage in marriage with that of Lady Emily Percy, granddaughter of the first Duke of Northumberland and daughter of the first Earl of Beverley. By this he was only continuing a pattern begun by previous generations of marrying into the aristocracy — "prosperity . . . owes as much to good marriages as good business" as the Drummonds wisely realised. They were already allied to the families of the Dukes of Rutland and St Albans; to the Earls of Oxford, Egmont, Northampton and Cholmondley, and to other lesser ranks of the nobility. Intermarriages between these families and unions between Drummond cousins were to produce a genealogy of enormous complexity, many Drummonds being related through both sides of their parentage. A number of these aristocratic relations of the Drummond children were portrayed in their drawings, along with equally illustrious friends. Many of the sketches were executed on the reverse of visiting cards bearing the names of yet more friends and relations who flitted in and out of their family life. Most were members of what was variously known as the "Polite" or "fashionable world", "Society", the *"Beau Monde"* or *"Haut Ton"*, and their leisure consisted of being in the right place at the right time. Broadly speaking this required being in London with the Court during the Season and the Parliamentary sessions and out of it when all was over. A country seat and a town house, or at the very least the rent of one, were essentials for membership of this world. Furthermore, whilst in London it was equally essential to have the entrée into one of the drawing rooms of the great political, literary or social centres, such as Devonshire House, Holland House, or Almacks — a club whose exclusiveness was legendary amongst those interested in such things. Admission to Almacks was granted by the handful of patronesses who ruled it, one of whom was Mrs Drummond-Burrell, another connection of the Drummond children. It was at Almacks that the favoured few assembled and danced, gossiped and gambled, and provided the etiquette

An Interior Scene.
More friends and relations. Left to right: The fashionable Mrs Beresford Hope, Louisa, Miss Burrowes, unnamed boy and Lady Gwydyr.
Signed Julia Frances Drummond. Watercolour $5\frac{7}{8}$" × 6".

Two more very young members of the family wearing the ubiquitous white frocks and coloured sashes of childhood, their hair carefully dressed and ornamented with sprigs of flowers.

Elizabeth, a very pretty young visitor.

for the rest of society to emulate. Harder to gain entry to than the court, its influence was said to reach far beyond the set which composed it. The magic of its reputation had already entranced one youthful Drummond who yearned for the time when she would be "dancing at Almacks balls". Writing in verse she begged her mother to:

> Take the hint and lead me to those halls
> Where youth assembles at so many balls

It was not only this young Drummond who was fascinated by Almacks. It was satirised in a novel of three volumes bearing its name, was "immortalised" by Cruikshank's drawings and referred to by both Thackeray and Disraeli in their novels.

Another leading light from their parents' world who appeared in the children's drawings was Lord Palmerston, also an habitué of Almacks. His flirtation with Lady Jersey, one of the patronesses, became the talk of the town. Though Lady Jersey was said to be delighted with her conquest, she nonetheless wanted to be thought of as a "dragon of virtue" and indeed boasted that she was "the

Detail from The interior of a drawing room in Brighton.
Mrs Beresford Hope, crowned in ribbons and tulle, elegantly reclining on a couch. The sleeves of her dress are in the latest à la Marie *fashion which succeeded those* en gigot.
Signed Julia Frances Drummond, 1828. Watercolour
$6\frac{15}{16}'' \times 9\frac{5}{16}''$.

most virtuous woman in England" — a sign perhaps that the moral revival of the rest of society was at last entering the conscience of the aristocracy.

The fashionable Mrs Beresford Hope, wife of the antiquarian and author, Thomas Hope of Deepdene, was another member of the circle. Painted by Lawrence, her name, eulogised *La Belle Assemblée*, that monthly record of the *Beau Monde*, was "associated . . . with all that was elegant and beautiful". She and Lady Gwydyr, both of whom appear in the drawings, had regular little *réunions*, as they called them, to play *écarté*, a card game at which, Lady Holland wrote, "even in the country 50 guineas could be lost in a moment". Mrs Hope's uncle and aunt, the Earl and Countess of Clare; Lady Georgiana Agar-Ellis; the Earl and Countess of Westmeath; Mrs Rigby (more famous subsequently as Lady Eastlake); Lady Emily Villiers; Lady Selby and Mrs Udny were other friends who drifted through the children's lives. Of relatives, there were Lady Agnes Buller, daughter of the second Duke of Northumberland and a cousin; Lady Gwydyr, sole heiress of Baron Drummond of Stobhall and related on both sides of the family through marriage. Her daughter Clementina and her small son Alberic appear in the drawings, as do the Earl and Countess of Ashburnham (their mother's sister), and Lady Hamilton (wife of Vice Admiral Hamilton and their father's sister), and also a number of unnamed adults and children, who it seems safe to say were likewise friends and relations.

About the Drummond children themselves: there were eight of them, seven daughters and one son, Mortimer, all born between 1810 and 1820. Mortimer was to turn out something of a

Interior Scene at Scotsbridge.
Two ladies wearing their carriage hats and bonnets appear to be paying a morning call to an invalided member
of the family, who is seated in a red striped chair with a medicine bottle on a table beside her. The lady on the
left of the chimneypiece is holding a fur tippet on her lap. The boned and tight lacing in the undergarments worn
by such ladies which prohibited stooping and bending is reflected in their erect bearing.
Signed C.E.D. 1830.

spendthrift, a throwback to his uncle George Drummond who went bankrupt. It was alleged that the first and only time George Drummond played whist he lost £20,000 in one night to Beau Brummel. Exiled to Dublin he lived there openly with his mistress, who styled herself Mrs Drummond. Mortimer's sisters were Emily-Susan, Eleanor-Charlotte, Julia-Frances, Cecil-Elizabeth, Agnes-Priscilla, Susan-Caroline and Marian. Cecil-Elizabeth, or Cecily as she was also called, married her cousin Heneage Drummond, who became a clergyman. Susan-Caroline married Heneage's brother Harvey. Both were brothers of Fanny Drummond. Agnes-Priscilla married another clergyman, the Reverend Berdmore Compton. Between these Drummond girls the credit of the drawings is shared, though the most accomplished was certainly the fourth daughter Cecil-Elizabeth, who continued painting watercolours in later life.

Some of the drawings are scenes at their country home at Denham in Buckinghamshire. It was a rather curious house as it consisted of two square brick Georgian mansions, one of which their father had pulled down when he bought the estate in 1819, and re-erected alongside the other. The rooms on the ground floor opened straight onto lawns, or through extended conservatories onto terraces, reflecting the current desire to be close to nature. There were thirty acres of land at the time of purchase, which over the years Andrew Mortimer Drummond increased to 560 acres. He also owned a town house, No 6 Grosvenor Place, and an estate at Roehampton, also with its own mansion. At Denham too, at The Fishery, lived some cousins. These were the children of their father's uncle, John Drummond, who, by his second marriage, had

children the same generation as themselves. It is from a collection of miscellaneous writings by his daughter Fanny, which were transcribed into an album by her mother (a former maid of honour to Queen Charlotte), that much of the information about the family is culled. It was this Fanny who yearned for Almacks balls when still a child.

Yet more cousins lived only four miles away at Scotsbridge, near Rickmansworth. Some of the drawings are of scenes in this house. These cousins were the children of their mother's brother, Vice Admiral the Honourable Josceline Percy. The "gallant" Admiral, who had served on Nelson's flagship the *Victory*, bought his estate in Hertfordshire in 1827. He had one son born in 1825, and three daughters.

For families like the Drummonds and their friends and relations, the cult of nature and the pleasures of the chase were pursued with an enthusiasm equal to that which they felt for London and the Season. When they quitted London they repaired to their estates or to one another's, to indulge in their concept of the pastoral idyll — "ruralizing", Lady Cowper called it. This meant hunting and shooting, boating and fishing, riding, driving or strolling through their own, or their friends', acres to admire the ubiquitous improvements with which this return to nature was marking the era. Additions and alterations to houses and grounds were all hailed as improvements and the profitable results which advances in agriculture and farming techniques yielded gave an additional impetus to the appreciation of nature.

Along with the improvement of their estates came a growing awareness of the poor wages and harsh conditions of those who laboured on them. The causes of rick burning and rioting

Untitled.
Left to right: Cecil (Cecil-Elizabeth), Clementina, Julia (Julia-Frances), Emily (Lady Emily Drummond?),
Lady Gwydyr, Elizabeth, Mme le Linwood and Augusta. In this delightful drawing of hatted and shawled
ladies, the two sisters, Cecil and Julia are dressed identically, and almost the same as their mother. Shawls of
cachemire de laine *were highly favoured, being the latest fashion and having superseded the rectangular ones*
of the first two decades.
Watercolour.

could no longer go unheeded and neither could the poverty of those who had drifted to the cities when starved out of the country. There in the cities, neglected by both Church and State, they had only the fervour of nonconformist religion and talk of radical politics for comfort. The groundswell of nonconformism to which this had given rise began to infect the rest of society. The small number of middle and upper-class reformers who had tried at the beginning of the century to work within the church, the Evangelicals, were, during the 1820s and 1830s, joined by an increasing number of the powerful middle classes also reacting against a lax, libertine and *laissez faire* establishment. This Evangelical movement took as its source book Henry Venn's *The Complete Duty of Man*, written in 1763, which was steeped in the Puritan tradition. Like its parent, the movement was rooted in the belief that it was the family above all that could and should generate a religious and moral attitude to life. Concerned more with humanitarian needs and saving souls than with doctrinal issues, its strength was amongst the laity — of whom the most influential "Saints", as Evangelicals became called, were Wilberforce, the Clapham Sect (of whom Hannah More was a leading member) and the Buxtons (Fowell Buxton aided Wilberforce in abolishing slavery). Evangelicals were instrumental in forming the Society for the Suppression of Vice and the Religious Tract Society. Theirs was a proselytising movement deeply committed to the importance of personal conversion. As Nancy Cutt has so clearly elucidated in her book on Mrs Sherwood, the children's author:

The whole outlook on life that is comprehended in the word "Victorian" is seen to be the widely-branching top of a living tree whose root is the Evangelical Movement. From Evangelicalism stemmed a missionary fervour that was not restricted to missions, a religious zeal that overflowed into politics. Evangelicalism was manifest in the urge to teach, preach and learn; to better oneself and to better the lot of others was a driving force, a motive power and a personal discipline.

Unlike its Puritan forebears, it managed to enlist, if gradually, many of the upper classes. In the sixteenth and seventeenth centuries the Puritans had little influence on courtly society, but in the nineteenth century the influence of the Evangelicals, aided by the general aura of evangelism rising up through society, was great enough to narrow this gap and change the ideals of "Polite" behaviour amongst the upper classes. Propriety or respectability was the secular image for correct behaviour and the importance which thereby became attached to external appearances was to lead to much of the hypocrisy for which the century became renowned. As the writer Lucy Aikin corroborates in 1834, the upper classes, "are much less addicted to drinking, less also to gaming for men play less . . . and women scarcely at all . . . there is much more decorum, much more of at least outward respectability for religion and virtue, and I think it is plain that even hypocrisy must put some restraint on vice."

Few people, regardless of their shade of religion, were to escape the influence of these reformers who were dedicated to making, as their critics described it, a moral domesticated society, devoid of philosophical or aesthetic interests. Princess Victoria, though neither she nor her mother were Evangelicals, became their exemplar, at least on the first two counts. She also fulfilled her mother's ambition for her. "Victoria is not to be fashionable, but is to acquire that equality of dignity that will affect all classes; I wish my daughter to be a pattern of female decorum as to example and *associates*." Likewise, there is no evidence that the Drummond family, exact contemporaries of the Princess, were Evangelicals either, but they were nevertheless also inextricably bound to the social mores of their day, and they, like many of their social equals, contrived, as Tawney said, to worship both Jesus and Mammon: one foot in the spiritual world and the other firmly in the material.

NURSERY YEARS

It was not surprising that Evangelicals should turn their attention to the upbringing of children. Where better to change society than through its young? Their main concern was of course the moral and spiritual welfare of the child, and their influence can be seen in some of the many child-care manuals which increasingly circulated from the beginning of the nineteenth century. These began to be characterised by an increasingly moral tone, and one of the issues which roused the greatest concern was that of infant feeding. The custom of hiring a wet-nurse was still prevalent amongst the upper classes, her employment being put down generally to the levity of the mother, who, in Rousseau's words, still preferred "the pleasures of the town" to the demands of her infant. This was blamed, together with a fear of spoiling the figure, and an inability to breast-feed caused by following a fashion which demanded "pernicious stays and stiff jackets". These circumstances gave rise to the heyday of the wet-nurse during the latter part of the eighteenth century. Though medical opinion considered it best for the welfare of both mother and child that the mother should feed her own infant, the prejudice against the wet-nurse in the nineteenth century was as much on moral grounds as physical. In the 1820s it was still believed that not only physical diseases were transmitted through breast milk, but also mental and moral qualities. A wet-nurse by her very calling was deemed immoral — 'fallen' — as most were unmarried. It was feared her moral deficiency would be passed on to the infant whom she suckled. Religious and moral pressure was brought to bear on mothers to awaken their maternal instincts and nurse their infants. Phrases telling them that it was a "sacred and delightful task", or their "duty" abounded. The success of these pleas is a moot point, for over thirty years later Trollope could still write: "Of course Lady Arabella could not suckle the young heir herself. Ladies Arabella never can. They are gifted with the powers of being mothers, but not nursing mothers. Nature gives them bosoms for show but not for use. So Lady Arabella had a wet-nurse."

It seems more than likely that there were some Ladies Arabella in the Drummond circle, as, like their eighteenth century predecessors, they were once again imprisoned in steel busks and tight stays.

Reformers were also at work on the altogether

6. Foley Place.

Untitled.
A small straw hatted girl pays a visit to an invalid,
sitting at a safe distance from her at the foot of the
half-tester bed. The drawing is one of a number
drawn on visiting cards. This card is inscribed Lady
Hamilton, who was the Drummond children's aunt.

diminishing role of the mother in her infant's upbringing, nurses having increasingly replaced her in the physical care of her infant. It was accepted regretfully that the father was only a background presence for the first ten years of his children's life: "Fashion decrees that anything to do with the nursery is 'voted a bore' by the modern, fine gentleman." Infancy and childhood were clearly designated women's work, and preferably the mothers'. These were urged to keep a closer watch over their nurses, for the high incidence of infant mortality — half the children born in 1831 died within the first five years, with the largest number of these under the age of two — was blamed mainly on neglect and mismanagement. Early death and disease was a fact no longer accepted either as inevitable, or as a hazard of poverty: all five of Queen Anne's children died in infancy, one in childhood and

many other pregnancies ended in miscarriages. Many untimely deaths were hastened by the malpractices of nurses which included passing the food through their own mouths first, ostensibly to make it more digestible and to render it the right temperature, a legacy from the eighteenth century when such practices were commonplace; administering the laudanum bottle to "'quieten infants' cries" (the laudanum bottle was the *sine qua non* of a nurse's furniture for, as one writer observed in 1827, "continual crying" was so common that it was erroneously thought natural to them, but is really due to bad management); and hand-feeding from dirty bottles with contaminated contents. These were still common occurrences in the first decades of the early nineteenth century, often causing gastroenteritis, the illness from which infants most frequently died.

Treatments seemed hardly better than the illness they were supposed to cure, as a glance at the prescription book of Mr Paine, a chemist of Rickmansworth, confirms. In this are several for the Percys of Scotsbridge, the Drummonds' cousins. Purgatives, for adults and children alike, appear most frequently, and it seems they were often not for the illness itself but to rid the patient of the poisons present in the medicines prescribed for the complaint. Master Percy was given a preparation containing mercury, probably to cure some feverish condition. This was followed by a strong dose of Epsom Salts, presumably to remove the mercury. His sister was prescribed a tonic draught twice a day which was made from one drachm of steel wine, twenty minims of tincture of iron chloride, and nine drachms of cinnamon water. Steel wine was prepared by digesting two ounces of iron filings in two pounds of sherry for a month. The tincture of iron chloride was probably to increase the iron intake without increasing the sherry, while the cinnamon water was for flavouring. The efficacy of these remedies, alas, is not recorded.

"Everybody, almost, in easy circumstances has a part of the house appropriated to what is called the nursery — often the least suitable," wrote Dr Dewees in 1825. Nurseries tended to be distant from parents' rooms, as Frances Power Cobbe, in her autobiography, recalled of her own, and near the attics as Mrs Norris reminds us in *Mansfield Park*. Barbara Charlton, a connection of the Drummonds, remembered the crowded conditions of her nursery where she slept in one room with her three brothers and sisters and two nurses. The room doubled in the daytime as a schoolroom with children of all ages together. In the drawing on page 28 a nurse holds an infant in her arms while listening to a small boy read aloud. An older girl is trying to read to herself and another is having a piano lesson, whilst the fashionable lady seems to be watching it all. It was this kind of scene which Elizabeth Ham, when a governess, found so intolerable, complaining bitterly of the noisy young children who, "too young to be my pupils were not thought too young to be turned into the schoolroom to play". The specialisation of rooms such as the ample children's wing or floor of the affluent Victorian home partly grew out of the inadequate accommodation of the 1820s.

For a mother, keeping a watchful eye on her nurse was not only a means to ensure the physical well-being of her infant, but also to protect her own authority and supremacy in the nursery. Rousseau, and Jacques Guille-

Untitled.
A rare and tender picture of a man with a small girl on his lap. Perhaps it is Andrew Mortimer Drummond with one of his young daughters.

The Schoolroom.
Though set in a gaily furnished room, this scene demonstrates the number of mixed activities going on at the same time and the corresponding noise which must have ensued. A nurse listens to a young boy practising his reading whilst holding an infant on her lap, an older girl is trying to concentrate on her work and another is having a music lesson. Their mother is paying a visit see how they are progressing.
March 29, 1828. Watercolour $6\frac{11}{16}$" × 9".

meau before him, warned in respect of the wet-nurse that the natural affection of the infant for its mother might be transferred to the nurse, a threat fully appreciated by one mother in the Percy milieu who wrote that "she can brook no rivalry in her nursery". When it did happen, mothers were driven to undesirable means to win back their infant's love, and would either, Rousseau said, dismiss the nurse or abuse her to the child to try to incur feelings of ingratitude in the child towards her. These, he predicted, would surely be turned in time on the mother herself. However, the pleasures of the *Beau Monde* and the demands of husbands outweighed such considerations in the eighteenth century, as they were to in the nineteenth, and hired attendants, ever more readily and cheaply available, continued to replace the parent for the greater part of the child's life. Into this, parents, or more often simply mothers, darted in and out, sometimes like colourful angels and at other times like dreaded tyrants, alternately meting out pleasures and punishments — as they can often be seen doing in the drawings here. By no means all nurses competed with parents for their children's affections, and the horrible Mrs Crabtree, immortalised in Catherine Sinclair's story *Holiday House*, had many real life counterparts, not least in Mrs Hawk who ruled the Cowper children's nursery with a "rod of iron". For Fanny Cowper, whose lonely childhood (despite brothers and a sister), was spent largely confined to her nursery with this unloved nurse, her fashionable mother's periodic invasions into her life brought unprecedented fun and gaiety, compensating for absences necessitated by her membership of Society. Barbara Charlton spoke of her and her sister's descent

into the dining room at Christmas to dine with their parents, grandfather, aunt and governess, as "an unforgotten landmark in our lives". Alas, instead of a place of amusement, which a nursery should be, it too often became a place of punishment by banishing children to it. For some children it was only on holidays, especially Christmas ones, that they emerged for any length of time from the obscurity of the nursery and enjoyed, as Frances Power Cobbe remembered, "Twenty or more people every day for meals, noisy and romping games played all over long corridors below the stairs and above; and, when older, charades, plays, masquerading and dancing." For young children of the upper classes the larger part of their early childhood was spent closeted in these nurseries, separated from servants, who were always presumed to corrupt, and from children not of their own class, whose influence was thought equally damaging. In former times children had been thrown into society to learn how to take their place. In the nineteenth century they were protected from it.

It was also during children's nursery years that their arduous spiritual journey began. Irrespective of the degree of piety to which their parents aspired, the growing tide of Evangelicalism exhorted parents to instill ideas of piety and spiritual knowledge into their children whilst still in infancy and to insist on the utmost discipline and filial obedience. The aim of childhood, wrote Mrs Chapone, was "to labour to enrich the mind with the essentials of Christianity, with piety, benevolence, meekness, humility, integrity and purity". This tide of religion and morality entered children's nurseries through an

A glimpse at her future self as a small girl tries on her mother's garland. Her dark purple dress presages the strong colours and stiff materials of which childrens' clothes were to be made in the coming decades.
Watercolour on card inscribed Lady Georgiana Agar-Ellis.

avalanche of literature directed at parents, governesses, nurses and children themselves. For adults there were tracts on sacred subjects and manuals and treatises on education, as well as those on health and child-care often couched in religious language and argued from a moral standpoint. More influential even in inculcating religious and moral ideas in children was the expanding field of literature for children. Perhaps not enough attention has been given, even today, to the significance of this field in shaping an epoch. Religious instruction formed the largest class of children's books between the sixteenth and nineteenth centuries and dominated their literature; today it is almost obsolete. For the very young the first moral lessons were in the form of ABCs with moral verses engraved beneath, or Mrs Trimmer's prints of sacred and profane subjects with explanations. These pioneered the teaching of small children through pictures. Her *History of the Robins*, a tale ostensibly to teach children how to care for birds, provided a metaphor for the correct relation of children to parents — one of complete dependence. Adults are always portrayed as virtuous by her and children wicked and, therefore, in need of saving — a view which Evangelicalism had revived. It was one that Mrs Sherwood shared. She was one of the most popular of all children's authors as she managed to wrap her didacticism up in tales which really appealed to them. Her story of *The Little Woodman and His Dog Caesar*, written for the very young, had every inducement for early religious and moral training: the Little Woodman's prayers are always answered. Anne Jemima Clough, sister of the poet Arthur Hugh Clough, wrote that religion took a deep hold of her mind as a result of listening before the age of twelve to her mother's friends discussing Evangelicalism and Low Church doctrine. Frances Power Cobbe again spoke for a number of children when she described her own religious experience: for her it was the sublime in religion which attracted her, rather like the awesomeness of thunder and storms, she said. Religion became a real pleasure to her, whereas she was dimly conscious of religious exercise being "more as a duty" for her parents. Her parents, in Evangelical language were "Under the Law", while with her the "New Life was already planted". This was before she was out of the nursery. Other children were less fortunate, and the indefatigable efforts of fervent proselytisers merely succeeded in "making religion repulsive to them ... surfeiting them with preaching, praying and tutorings".

THE SCHOOLROOM
OR EDUCATION AT HOME

IT WAS THROUGH education that the Evangelicals could see their beliefs being most successfully transmitted, and what was begun in the nursery continued to the schoolroom. With unremitting energy and zeal they disseminated these beliefs through teachers and tutors, text-books and tracts until they, or those whom they influenced, commanded a very substantial part of the educational press. The printed word became their most powerful means of expression.

Hannah More, second only to Wilberforce as the secular force behind Evangelicalism, addressed herself in some of her many proselytising works to those of "rank and fortune". For, like Locke before her, she believed that "if those of that rank [gentlemen] are once by their education set right, they will quickly bring all the rest in order". Class distinctions were no hurdles either to Locke or to Evangelicalists. "Rank and fortune" were clearly God given — a fact made plain by this pronouncement of the Vicar of St Swithins: "It clearly manifests Divine Wisdom in the economy of Providence, that civil society should be composed of subordinate as well as superior classes."

The Evangelicals' aim was to reverse the rational and material bases on which education in the eighteenth century had been founded and which, in their view, had led to religious indifference, atheism, and revolution. The broad tenets of their teaching were, in addition to creating a family-dominated society, the encouragement of strict religious observance, moral excellence, industry and effort. Religion and duty were to be the new ethos rather than rights and reason. Religion was the first principle of all education — a belief shared by all shades of religious opinion, and one fully instilled in Fanny Drummond who felt "religion should mingle with everything, should give motive to exertions, solemnity to punishment and add pleasure to reward". Within this framework each sex must cultivate "those talents and accomplishments appropriate to itself". For girls, "born to submit to the authority of men", their education was to fit them to be daughters, wives, mothers and mistresses of families because, as Hannah More continued, "domestic life is to woman her proper sphere".

Girls like the Drummonds received this education mainly within the confines of home, where they were safely preserved from undesirable influences, namely contact with in-

Untitled.

Left to right: Henry, Arthur, Ben, Louisa (Lady Ashburnham) and Tommy. The young men, perhaps down from university, pay a visit to a schoolroom, suggested here by the large globe. Studying the globe was an important part of the schoolroom curriculum, reflecting the growing interest in other parts of the world due to the expansion of the empire.

Inscribed 'When I was 16.' Signed C.E.D. February, 1830. Watercolour $5\frac{1}{16}'' \times 7\frac{3}{8}''$.

ferior persons or members of the opposite sex. Though the plan of domestic education was said to have been universally adopted by 1831, this was some exaggeration since private boarding schools continued to exist especially as precursors of the finishing school. Girls who, on reaching fifteen or sixteen, did not have a "finishing" governess were often sent to such schools to acquire the accomplishments and "training in the Great Art of Society" as described by Frances Power Cobbe, herself sent to school for that purpose. Despite the disapproval of the moralists, pretensions to piety did not preclude parents from wishing their daughters to become ornaments of the drawing room and often with a pragmatism worthy of their fashionable mentor, Lord Chesterfield, they contrived to reconcile the demands of the "polite" world with those of the "spiritual". The ideal, as the Reverend Gurney wrote in his memoir of his daughter, was "to attain the best tone of religious feeling with the highest polish". Accomplishments were a mark of good breeding and leisure. Thus they were necessary not only as a relief from the *ennui* of too much spare time, but also as a means of securing a good marriage. Even Hannah More conceded that fashionable customs, when not hostile to "virtue, should unquestionably be pursued in the education of ladies". They were energetically taught for those reasons rather than as attributes in their own right. "Everything", complained Frances Power Cobbe, "was taught in reverse ratio of its true importance and any ambition to become an artist or an author was considered a deplorable dereliction." Hannah More, who had the philistinism of the Puritan in her fear of the arts, saw their cultivation as a source of corruption for women, diverting them from their true domesticity. "The pursuit of accomplishments is only justified if forming a branch of moral discipline by trying the temper and exercising the patience," both in her view and in the words of a member of the Drummond family.

Whilst girls were endeavouring to acquire that "best tone of religious feeling and the highest polish", boys were aiming for "a moral and political knowledge — the proper concern of a gentleman". They were to be served by habits of piety, principle, courage and learning, qualities similar to Locke's virtue, wisdom, breeding and learning, the four endowments of a gentleman. Until the age of ten, boys and girls shared their education, after which boys either remained at home studying with a tutor or more often were sent away to public school, preferably one of the older ones attended by those of the same rank in society as themselves to ensure that their friends were their social equals. For if one's class was ordained, so it seems was one's rank within that class, as Prince Pückler-Muskau, a shrewd observer of the English scene, was quick to notice.

> The spirit of *caste*, which ... descends through all stages of society in greater or less force, has received here a power, consistency and full development, wholly unexampled in any other country ... No Brahmin can shrink with more horror from contact with a Paria than an "Exclusive" from intercourse with a "Nobody". Each has his own manners and terms of expression — its "cant" language as it is called — and above all a supreme contempt for all below it.

Education, therefore, should fit one's expected station in life.

Untitled.
Tears over lessons were all too common.
Watercolour on card inscribed Lady Agnes Buller.

A Scene in the Blue Room.
This sketch shows the children being put through their paces on a visit to the drawing room.
Stamped Cecil, July 11, 182–. Watercolour $5\frac{5}{8}$″ × $7\frac{5}{16}$″.

Surprisingly then, it is to Princess Victoria, the Drummond girls' contemporary, that one has to turn to get a closer picture of their own education. When the Princess was approaching thirteen the Duchess of Northumberland was appointed her governess to oversee her education. Saying that she had been "guided by the customary system adopted in education by young females in this country" she proposed a scheme based on this, broadening it to meet the requirements of the Princess's own exalted position and expectancy. To inform the Duchess of Kent, the Princess's mother, what this system entailed she sent her the reading lists of several girls of her acquaintance of similar age including two of her own nieces, one of whom, Louisa-Julia Percy, was a cousin of the Drummond children. Sacred works dominated these lists, with historical and biographical coming next; these were followed by drama, poetry and literature, both French and English; geography and the use of the globes; astronomy, botany or natural history; arithmetic; and French and English grammars. Many works were read twice and much was learnt by heart. History and religious knowledge for children were often written in the form of catechisms and memorised, as were, at times, entire grammars of foreign languages. Rote rather than reason was the keynote, for, as the author Lucy Aikin wrote in 1832, "women are seldom taught to *think*", perhaps because encouraging them might lead them to think differently. In keeping with this attitude was the complete absence of novels in the reading lists, again marking the Puritan distrust of the imagination, a characteristic inherited by the Evangelicals. Not one novel was included in the Duchess of Northumberland's own proposals

for Princess Victoria's reading. She had to wait until she was a queen for that pleasure. Her children's books were gradually to be replaced by travel, biography, poetry and letters for her leisure hours to give both "delight and instruction". Pleasure alone was not a part of the Evangelical programme, and neither was it to be for Princess Victoria. Novels and romances were doubly taboo, as Mrs Chapone explained in her letters of advice to her fifteen-year-old niece. "They inflame the passions of youth when the chief purpose of education is to moderate and restrain them." It was also feared that fiction in any form might instil a craving for narrative when it was more important to instil truth in the mind than imagination. Maria Edgeworth disapproved of *Robinson Crusoe* fearing it might lead to a taste for adventure, especially amongst young boys: a surprising stricture for a supposed follower of Rousseau, who had heartily recommended the book to young readers. Even the fashionable Walter Scott was taken to task for his novel writing, whilst he himself deplored this current attitude to the imagination, fearing its result would be "no wits or orators" in the next generation.

The Princess's week was to be rigidly time-tabled, a pattern for her contemporaries. Each day was to begin with some learning by heart accomplished before breakfast, after which the psalms for the day and an extract from Mrs Trimmer's Bible were to be read. This was to be followed by five hours of study interrupted only for lunch and walking. Saturdays would provide a slight variation, in that the week's work was examined in the morning with the rest of the day devoted to letter writing, dancing lessons and "tasks" — an ominous word, which carried a "train of melancholy ideas"

associated with it. Sunday, of course, would have its own character. Until the Princess's confirmation, it was to begin with learning the Collect of the Day before breakfast and repeating it after, together with the catechism. After Morning Service the Princess would write down the "pearls" from the sermon and in the afternoon read the Evening Service and a so-called Sunday Book. These would be works of instruction such as volumes of sermons and special editions of the psalms or other works which she would find "amusing without being trivial". In that category came Milton's *Paradise Lost*, Thomson's *Seasons*, Gray's *Elegy*, and *The Life of Zwingli*, the Swiss reformer. Optimistically, the Duchess suggested that Sunday should "never be a day of gloom but one of religious instruction blended with chearful [sic] domestic relaxation". However, it was these joyless misrepresentations of piety which made religion a duty rather than a pleasure and "stamped this day with a sort of death-like character". As another of the Princess's contemporaries said, "the horror of Sunday used even to cast its prescient gloom as far back in the week as Friday — and all the glory of Monday, with church seven days removed again, was no equivalent for it".

Unlike the Princess, who was to be taught by masters who were implicitly of a higher academic calibre than women, the Drummonds and girls like them received their education from a governess and at times a conscientious parent, with perhaps the occasional visiting teacher. Governesses were, on the whole, an exploited and unhappy class of women, whose calling was generally the result of some misadventure not of their own making. Like the fictional governess in Fanny

Untitled.
More tears as a Mother remonstrates with her small daughter over her lessons. An older one continues her practise whilst her younger brother carries on with his reading. Their governess is about to open the door, presumably to send the crying child away.
Ascribed to Cecil Elizabeth Drummond, April 1829. Watercolour $7\frac{5}{8}'' \times 9''$.

Interior Scene at Scotsbridge.
In this the lady in the riding habit is a reminder that women had ridden to hounds since the earliest days of the chase. However the long skirts of their habits, which had to be carried over the arm until the wearer was mounted, made jumping difficult when riding side-saddle — the position in which women rode. Petticoats and pantaloons were worn beneath these habits, which were made by men's tailors.
Signed C.E.D. Monday, March 20th, 1830. Watercolour $7\frac{5}{16}'' \times 9''$.

Drummond's own essay in remembrance of her education, they were mostly daughters of unsuccessful professional men thrown into taking such situations by a world which considered that the "most enlarged view of charity was for every individual to provide for himself, so as to prevent himself becoming a burden on society", a revealing glimpse of contemporary Christianity. These unfortunate women, often with little education themselves, "sought a respectable asylum in the nurseries of the opulent who in turn fell upon them since they were gentlewomen and therefore nearer to what they could wish their children to become". The weariness of their existence has been captured, not only in fiction as in Charlotte Bronte's *Shirley*, inspired by her own unhappy experiences as a governess, but also in memoirs of those who had been brought up by governesses and in the journals and recollections of governesses themselves. Barbara Charlton describes her own governess's position in the household as one which was "considered too low to keep us company in the drawing room and too high for association with the servants". A governess was expected to be deeply committed to her own spiritual improvement as well as that of her pupil; lip service was not enough. She was cheerfully reminded, that "life is a battle to be fought; a race to be run, a labour to be performed. The rest for the people of God is not to be enjoyed in this world; in death alone is Victory". By 1861, when reform in education for girls was beginning to be demanded, Harriet Martineau neatly, if brutally, summed up the whole governess system: "The time must surely be nearly at an end when parents can save the expense of school-going for their whole batch of daughters, including sons under ten-years-old, by engaging a young lady on the wages of a nursemaid ... attempting to teach what she never properly learned."

PUNISHMENT AND CORRECTION

FOR MANY CHILDREN satisfying the sometimes excessive demands of their parents and preceptors was often a painful process. The prevailing attitude that children's natures were inherently directed towards evil, rather than good, implied a need for continual correction. Rousseau and the Romantics had believed in the innocence of childhood while many of the increasingly influential new Puritans preached the harsh doctrine of their forebears, a doctrine of original sin. For instance Hannah More asked, "is it not a fundamental error in Christians to consider children as innocent beings, rather than as beings who bring into the world a corrupt nature and evil disposition which it should be the great aim of education to rectify". She urged that educators "make aware the knowledge of the corruption of our nature and create within us the desire to correct it". Mrs Sherwood reiterated her views recommending any means of correction. "All children are by nature evil," she declared, "pious and prudent parents must check their naughty passions in any way they have in their power and force them into decent and proper behaviour." Thus it was necessary to create a system to repress, restrain and rectify children's natural propensities for evil, so

replacing Rousseau's desire to bring them up in freedom and liberty. Obedience, that foundation stone of Evangelical teaching, was precisely one of the concepts which, together with command, duty and obligation, Rousseau would have liked deleted from the vocabulary concerning children. For the Evangelicals obedience was a "prerequisite of faith"; as the *Father's Eye* explained: "Our natural parents are the same to us in our infancy as God and our Church are to the believer in and after life and hence the little child who is taught to love, honour and obey his parents, to trust in them and to submit wholly to their wills, is as well prepared as sinful man can be, for that state of dependence on his heavenly Father in which all human wisdom doth consist."

For parents influenced by this religious tradition it was a licence to enforce rigorous discipline and correction upon their children, often a licence to cruelty. The Drummond children's drawings are a witness to the stringent and severe measures resorted to by their own parents. Beneath the seductive gaiety of bright colours their drawings reveal, with disarming candour, scenes of punishment and pain. They have recorded themselves being "drilled" and weeping over their lessons, being severely reprimanded, being beaten and forced into wearing painful back-boards. Their parents clearly subscribed to the belief that punishment is good for children. In the sixteenth and seventeenth century punitive beatings were considered an essential part of education, a divine duty instituted by God, who in his wisdom and providence even fashioned the human posterior in such a manner that no lasting injury was sustained by it! Beatings were administered with a ceremony intended to shame the offender as much as to pain him. Gradually doubt grew as to the efficacy of this form of punishment, for it too often caused rebellion in the victim and loss of control in the punisher — a sign of the repressed sadism which the act of beating unleashed in its perpetrator. One author, writing against corporal punishment in 1822, argued with much perspicacity that beatings were "too often given according to the rage excited in our breasts rather than according to the crime committed". "Trivial offences," he related, "such as a blot in a copy book, a stammering in reading, a spelling mistake or for not answering immediately were punished by beating."

In fact, since the end of the eighteenth century corporal punishment had ceased to be approved as a universal method, instead most of the tracts on education rather uneasily recommended it as a last resort to use when all else failed. Their tenor of thought was expressed in the following passage from a contemporary tract: "It [the rod] should be administered as a chastisement of the most serious nature with decision, perfect serenity of temper, and affection towards the offender." Unfortunately, as the previous writer had observed, parents and teachers continued to be unable to distinguish between the serious and the trivial with the result that beatings, both at home and school, remained a common practice. It is hard to imagine that the Drummond children were guilty of anything more serious than the trivial offences mentioned above.

However, not all educationalists shared the dismal view of children's nature, in which punishment was an inevitable part of correction. There was no corporal punishment in schools run on the lines recommended by the contemporary Swiss educationalist, Pestalozzi. Maria Edgeworth, in *Practical Education*, written jointly with her father, stated that "if children are reasonably and affectionately educated scarcely any punishment will be requisite" — an insight made long before psychology was to illuminate for us children's behaviour and needs. The Edgeworths, though stern moralists, left religion, and religious instruction as a subject, out of their scheme of education, teaching instead that virtuous behaviour might be achieved through good example rather than by precepts and rules — a Lockeian view and one which contrasted with religion's stress on the importance of precept. "The practice of setting examples before young people for their imitation, is not so efficacious in forming them to the higher virtues as nourishing their minds with noble precepts", wrote Lucy Aikin, in contrast to Maria Edgeworth's view that the fewer rules the better. Obedience too, for her was only a relative rather than a positive virtue, again a contrast to the Evangelicals for whom it was fundamental and to be achieved by force if necessary. Maria Edgeworth urged that obedience should be encouraged by showing that it produced happiness for the child. Prevention was better than correction, and if

Untitled.
A backboard in use. One of the painful devices for
straightening young children's backs.
Watercolour on card inscribed Mrs Rigby.

punishment was necessary, it was only to be given for the hurt it had done to others, and as a deterrent to those who might do likewise. The best way of instilling truthful and moral behaviour was "to associate pleasure with all that was good and pain with what should be avoided". This should be accompanied by benevolent and affectionate kindness from parents to children and by "children giving pleasure to one another" — a rare thought. Few educationalists had bothered to take account of children's relationships with one another; nor for that matter had history. Parent-children relations were the only ones deemed important. Though Maria Edgeworth did not share Rousseau's optimism that children, if allowed to exercise their free will, would naturally choose the path of virtue, she nevertheless had more in common with his and Locke's approach, one which also held childhood to be a state worthy of respect, than with the overzealous religious moralists for whom childhood was merely a stage for the preparation of adulthood.

Both approaches were fused in Fanny Drummond's long essay which she also titled "Practical Education", a memorial to her sister's and her own upbringing. Like her mentors she had the same obsessive pre-occupation with moral development and the character-forming aspects of education. Through a set of moral tales, after the manner of Mrs Sherwood, she creates situations in which two young sisters display various acts of disobedience, obstinacy, temper and so on, and tells of psychological pressures and disciplines which their governess and mother brought to bear on them to force them into a state of contrition, humility and repentance. For example, each night slates were placed

Detail from A Scene at Scotsbridge.
This looks very much as if it is the same little girl who was crying on pages 36 and 39. This time she has refused to wear her backboard, which lies discarded at her feet. She seems about to be birched for this deed by her mother, and stands weeping at her scolding.
Signed C.E.D. Thursday, April 1st, 1830.
Watercolour 7" × 8".

beside their beds for them to fill with self-examining questions and entreaties. Self-knowledge, self-control, self-examination were all aids which Puritans believed would help along the path of virtue. The children suffered punishment mainly in the form of deprivations, the common replacements for beatings. These were mostly of the nature of withdrawal of either approval (a Lockeian form of punishment) or of a prized possession, or the prohibition of some pleasure, such as a visit to the drawing room. Many such punishments were combined with a spell of solitary confinement, during which the child should reflect on her misdeed until she shed tears of shame. Much was made of the all-seeing eye of God which saw children's most secret thoughts, an idea which inflamed children's sense of guilt. Finally, all behaviour was recorded in a Conduct Book by their governesses, to be read monthly to their mothers.

The Conduct Book was another means of coercing children into good behaviour, in the hope that the knowledge that their behaviour was being recorded for some day of judgement a month hither would keep them good. Princess Victoria had Conduct Books which she was obliged to keep herself. Her behaviour did appear to improve, for her first book in 1831 was full of entries like "impertinant [sic], naughty, vulgar, thoughtless, foolish [sic], *very very* naughty", with few entries of "good" or "pretty good". But by 1833 she was able to write a whole day in which her conduct was almost exemplary: "Pretty good behaviour, very good behaviour, very good lesson, pretty behaviour, odd behaviour." Her behaviour books which were charted, just like a timetable for lessons, make delightful reading, something which she, her mother, or the Duchess of

Northumberland were unlikely to have anticipated.

Children were also expected to express their gratitude and dependence on their parents through their prayers and verses, and prayers of parental praise were almost as ubiquitous as those in praise of God, the following from Princess Victoria being typical examples: "Make me dutiful to my adored Mamma," she prayed; or, "Let me show by my good conduct, to dear Mamma, how grateful I am for all she does for me." And in the following letter to her mother she expressed the ideal relationship to themselves, which parents desired of their children:

> Dearest Mamma, I must thank you for your great kindness to me and I hope to repay it by being a good and obedient child to my dearest Mamma, I hope never any more to hear Mamma say "I am shocked" but to hear her say "I am pleased". I am your very dutiful and very obedient, and affectionate daughter, Victoria.

Often this gratitude was worked on samplers, as in this verse from Sarah Harrison's sampler to her parents:

> Next to God dear Parents I address
> Myself to you in humble thankfulness
> For all the care on me bestow'd
> And mean of learning under me allowed.
> Go on dear parents let me still pursue
> Those golden arts the vulgar never knew.

Written essays, whilst being exercises in literacy, were also vehicles for instilling moral lessons. "Why should you always speak the Truth" was the title of one which the young Elton boys had to write.

In short, as one author put it, children's education of that period was conditioned by the "incessant repetition of moral saws".

Correction also implies physical correction and the back-boards worn by the small Drummond girls are a reminder of the importance which was attached to outward appearance. Just as moral or good behaviour was reflected by good manners, so good breeding was expressed by an elegant deportment. As a contemporary voice from Almacks proclaimed, "The distinguishing mark of gentility consisted in a certain grace and ease of deportment proceeding from an early and continued cultivation of the figure and action alike, remote from vulgarish constraints." The ideas of moral rectitude and physical erectness were inevitably fused. To aid deportment in the eighteenth century children had been subjected to a number of straightening and strengthening devices of which the back-board, amongst others, lingered on, despite growing criticism from the medical profession and other educators about the efficacy of such contrivances. Iron collars, stocks for the feet, slanting boards, neck-swings in which children were suspended whilst their stays were tightly laced, were some of the more tortuous contraptions. Mrs Sherwood described how from the age of six until twelve she had to wear an iron collar around her neck with a back-board strapped to her back, and how she generally had to do all her lessons standing up wearing it. It was put on in the morning and only removed late in the evening. Mrs Hartford, in Lucy Aikin's memoirs, recalls similar experiences of her own childhood.

Dancing had also long been a recognised means of acquiring correct deportment, and it was the dancing master who taught the com-

The same small girl last seen on page 30 happily trying a wreath of flowers in her hair is now tearfully clutching a handkerchief in anticipation of the punishment she will receive for discarding her backboard, like the child in the last picture. A birch rod lies ominously ready on the shelf in front of her. Watercolour on card inscribed Countess of Clare.

plicated salutations in the mannered society of the seventeenth and eighteenth centuries. As Steele described in the *Spectator*, "No sooner is a girl safely brought from her nurse than she is delivered to the hands of her dancing-master and with a collar around her neck the pretty wild thing is taught a fantastical gravity of behaviour." For in the polite world, children, when in the company of adults, were expected to behave as demure miniatures of their seniors. The virtues of dancing had been extolled by Locke, who thought that "nothing appears, to me, to give Children so much becoming Confidence and Behaviour ... manly Thoughts and Carriage". Lord Chesterfield, whose precepts for the Polite world were still a paradigm in the 1830s, said that he "never knew anybody dance very well who was not genteel in other things". He wrote to his son saying he would do nothing with regard to his bodily carriage and address, but leave them to the care of his dancing-master. The dancing-master had even held a Court office. His reign reached its zenith at the end of the eighteenth century when an influx of *Maîtres de Danse*, refugees from the French Revolution came to England, and continued to teach the deportment and manners of a society which the French Revolution had swept away. But dancing as a courtly art declined and with it the mannered behaviour of previous centuries. In the nineteenth century the *Maître de Danse* at Almacks lamented that it was only girls who still had dancing lessons, young men considering such things unmanly. No longer were dancing and fencing the accomplishments to form a gentleman; instead innumerable academies of gymnastics sprang up, and exercises or callisthenics became the fashionable methods of straightening children to give them a proper bearing. Prince Pückler-Muskau wished he was a child again so as to be able to take all the advantages offered. So many facilities were "at hand for the physical as well as the moral education of man". He tells us how "those whom nature has mis-shapen are placed within cases of iron until they are transformed into Apollos". Not only boys enjoyed these advantages, for feminine gymnastics were just as popular, again much to the disgust of the *Maître de Danse* of Almacks. He put the popularity with females down to the need to correct the mischief created by the stupidity of the current fashion, that of "a smaller waist than nature has designed the person". Young females were laced to such a degree of tightness that their health was at risk, and exercises were resorted to in order to counteract the damage brought about by the excessive fashions. Though how girls could carry them out under such conditions he could not imagine. He wrote of the inappositeness of exercises for women and stressed the importance of being a graceful dancer. Awkwardness and slovenliness of gait and gesture were incompatible with high birth and rank. Girls must learn to have a dignified and gentle bearing reflecting their femininity and dependence; the image which the nineteenth century wished to have of their women.

Untitled.
Older girls were also punished, and here both parents are seen admonishing their stylish daughter with her upswept hair. She also has dissolved into tears and appears to have been ordered from the room.

Indoor Scene on Good Friday.
A surprising occupation for Good Friday. However practising the steps for the Quadrille which Fanny wrote
"is now all the rage" does not appear to have been precluded by the solemnity of the day. Note the way in which
a large square of carpet has been lifted away to make room for the dancers. Rugs or carpets were often laid loose
in this manner. The lady sitting on the right in her blue ruched bonnet, wears a very fashionable white ground
cachemire de laine *shawl with coloured border attached to her hand.*
Signed C.E.D. April 17, 1829.

LEISURE AND PLEASURE

LIKE THEIR PARENTS, the Drummond children also had their hours of leisure and pleasure, if not as many. And like the Ancients, their parents believed that "nature not only requires us to work well but to idle well". The children spent some of their free time idling in the best ways suited to their years, and some in preparing for the leisure hours of their adulthood, in which accomplishments would be essential to social advancement.

Though dancing had ceased to be a courtly art, and, as discussed in the last chapter, the influence of the dancing-master had subsequently declined, its popularity as a form of amusement remained undiminished. For girls, especially, it was also an indispensable social asset. "A girl who danced well was most taken notice of in public, and most likely to have her choice not only of the best partner in the ballroom but the best partner for life." That the Drummonds appear to have agreed with this view is evidenced here in the delightful drawing of both small girls and older ones practising their steps for the Quadrille which they can be seen dancing overleaf. The Quadrille was first danced at Almacks in 1816, brought over from Paris by the redoubtable Lady Jersey. Immensely popular, it was only surpassed by the waltz which, though it had crossed the Channel slightly earlier, had been greeted by cries of indignation, owing, in the words of *The Times*, to its "voluptuous intertwining of limbs, and close compressure of the bodies" — the "close-hold". First danced in Society at Court (also in 1816), *The Times* could only regret this "evil example" which was to be "forced on the respectable classes by their Superiors". It went on to "warn every parent against exposing his daughter to so evil a contagion".

Hitherto, as Mozart so perfectly illustrated at Zerlina's wedding in *Don Giovanni*, only peasants waltzed. Aristocrats danced the minuet. However the irresistible rhythms and seductive tunes of the waltz soon overcame most qualms and waltzing mania took hold; the waltz became for the nineteenth century what the minuet had been for the eighteenth. This was a defeat for the moralists especially at a time when outward appearances were so important. Dancing with the opposite sex was in any case feared by the Puritans for the danger of arousing improper passions. Quakers and Methodists did not allow dancing in any form and Evangelicalists, like Wilberforce

The Ball or Dancing lesson.
Probably a family party rather than a lesson. The young girls are wearing evening dresses with short sleeves en beret, *which some have covered with long gauze ones,* décolleté *necklines and full skirts. Their hair is elaborately dressed and ornamented with flowers or ribbons. The older ladies wear evening hats. The young men wear light coloured trousers strapped under their shoes, despite the efforts of the patronesses of Almacks to retain breeches for ballroom wear. They are dancing to the violin, the player being the young man in the brown coat, third from the left.*
Ascribed to Cecil-Elizabeth Drummond. September 28. Watercolour 7" × 9".

Untitled.
On the facing page two very young couples whirl together. In the small sketch an elderly gentleman, still wearing the no longer fashionable breeches is about to sit down under a tree.
Watercolour on card inscribed Earl of Ashburnham.

and Hannah More, disapproved of it. "Even before," as Hannah More reminded her readers in the 1830 edition of her works, "the indecent and offensive waltz had been added to the amusements of our virtuous ladies." Others, like the tract-makers, joined the protest, and Lord Byron wrote a satirical poem called *The Waltz: an Apostrophic Hymn*, in which he drew attention to its "lewd grasp and lawless contact warm". Mrs Sherwood, who had enjoyed dancing in her own youth, thanked God that her daughters had never asked her permission to enter the ballroom since the waltz had taken over from the minuet. Helped by Thomas Wilson who, in promoting the waltz, assured the world that it "held no dangers for morals or virtues", it soon ceased to be the graceful measured dance it had been. According to an observer at Almacks it became "a frenzied gallop, a rapid romping rambling dance, a fashionable scamper, and an excuse for a *tête à tête*". But the seal of respectability was given by the "correct" Queen Adelaide, who was said by Creevey to be an excellent waltzer. Thus the go-ahead was signalled for Princess Victoria — providing, of course, that she was partnered only by men of Royal blood.

In two thumbnail sketches two Drummond couples can be seen whirling away long before the girls could have been old enough to Come Out, the great moment of her life for a girl in Society. The term meant launching her into the world, the Polite World, and when once launched she might whirl around four or five ballrooms a night, as did Cecilia Ridley, a contemporary of the Drummonds. Until then a girl's appearance at an adult ball was rare, even though baby balls or children's balls had become the order of the day. However, judg-

ing from contemporary comment, they were received with more pleasure by their parents than by the children, who had to appear elaborately dressed, well-rehearsed in their steps, and required to conduct themselves with the composure of adults. "Their invention," Hannah More said, "was a triple conspiracy against the innocence, health, and happiness of children." She would of course have been prejudiced against them in any case, though this time others agreed with her. According to Prince Pückler-Muskau, "The only natural feeling displayed on these occasions was parental pride, displayed in the tenderness of their mothers' gaze." Describing one such ball, given not suprisingly by Lady Jersey, he said:

It really afflicted me to see how early they had ceased to be children; the poor things were for the most part as unnatural, as unjoyous, and as much occupied with themselves as we great figures around them ... it was only at supper that the animal instinct displayed itself more openly and unre-

A Game of Charades.

A game frequently played by adults, as in this picture. Taking part from left to right are: Louisa, The Major, Lord Palmerston, Papa, (Andrew Mortimer Drummond) Mrs Beresford Hope, Lady Westmeath, Miss Burrowes, Young Annabelle and Lady Gwydyr. Mrs Hope always in the forefront of fashion appears to be wearing a false piece of hair on the top of her head, erected on wire and with ringlets over her temples. This may be the "Apollo knot" style, popular for evening wear. Lady Westmeath is wearing an evening gown with long gauze sleeves over her short 'beret' ones, as does Louisa.

September 28.

54

The Cockfight.
In this visit to the drawing room two young men are playing a popular duelling game. In this version the two opponents are playing it on hunkers — that is in a squatting or crouching position with their hands clasped under their knees. One of them has already been toppled, the object of the contest. The girl in white bending over the fallen contender appears to be umpiring, whilst the other young members of the company are taking little interest and are occupied in talking to their Mothers or visitors.
Signed C.E.D. Monday, August 31, 1829. Watercolour $7\frac{7}{18}'' \times 9''$.

servedly and breaking through all forms and disguises and re-instated nature in her right.

The King gave such balls and, as fashion was the undisputed goddess in England, parents were indefatigable in conforming to her dictates.

There were also other accomplishments, equally important as dancing, "supposed to increase a young lady's chance of a prize in the matrimonial lottery". Little else could enlarge a girl's sphere more than a passable performance on the keyboard and a charming voice. These social accomplishments have been inimitably described by Jane Austen in *Emma*. Again the Drummond children's upbringing can be seen conforming to the convention of their day as they struggle with their keyboard exercises. However, there were some less than enchanted with the results of such efforts: "To be present at a musical soirée is one of the severest trials to which foreigners in England can be exposed," complained Prince Pückler-Muskau once more. "Every mother who has grown-up daughters, for whom she has to pay large sums to the music master, chooses to have the youthful 'talent' admired. There is nothing, therefore, but the quavering and strumming from right and left, so that one is really overpowered and unhappy." He was no more complimentary about masculine talents, though found their lack of ability which they "combined with a far greater confidence than a David", more diverting. There were of course times of pure spontaneous pleasure as Frances Power Cobbe recalled of her own childhood. These were during the great family occasions of Christmas and Easter when errant parents of the Polite World returned to indulge their children to make up for their absences, and older brothers and sisters finished school or came down from university. Lady Cowper (Fanny Cowper's mother, another patroness of Almacks and future wife of Lord Palmerston), was an exemplar of this kind, entertaining her children at such times, and exerting herself "manfully or rather womanfully, to make the dear children pass a merry Christmas". She gave, as she liked to describe them, brilliant balls each New Year as part of the Christmas celebrations, where grown-ups and children danced together. The Drummonds did likewise at Easter and, like the Cowpers, played games of all sorts every night.

Even moralists allowed some amusement "for it helps us to perform our duties" said Henry Thornton, a relation of Wilberforce, a friend of Hannah More, and a member of their Clapham Sect. Throughout the nineteenth century childish amusements such as practical jokes and games based on hiding, seeking, duelling, guessing and chance were popular with children and adults alike. From the outpourings of wicked epigrams, a favourite pastime of Lady Caroline Lamb's circle in the early part of the century, to the puerile games played by the Pooters and their acquaintances at the end of it the pattern remained the same. In this league was the kind of joke which the Drummonds played with false books. It was a common practice to conceal a door in a library by sticking the backs of books onto it, so that the line of bookshelves would not be interrupted. At the Tile House instead of these false books having real titles and authors, they bore false ones all of which referred to some family joke or event, though what these were has sadly not been recorded.

In the Great Houses, in the early nineteenth century, amateur theatricals were also a fashionable pastime, and even in Evangelical circles there were fancy dress parties for the young. Hannah More actually wrote the script for a puppet show which was performed at one. There were games like charades which included children and were played here by the Drummonds and their friends, one of whom was the pleasure-loving young Palmerston. Other games popular with boys, or young men, were duelling ones such as cockfight — a traditional game which came in many forms, from contests with conkers to trials of strength between two opponents, trying, as here, to put each other off balance — whilst the younger children's time-honoured games such as Blind Man's Buff continued to hold their fascination. As the Opies pointed out in their work on children's games, the idea of a chaser being so disadvantaged through not seeing is irresistible to children's minds. Locke discerned that children must have recreation and that "there can be no *Recreation* without delight". The Drummond children were fortunate to be able to play games as rumbustious as Blind Man's Buff — a welcome contrast to the rigours of their schoolroom life. Less fortunate were children brought up in extreme Puritan homes where pleasure was regarded as a sin: homes like Ruskin's, whose mother's particular brand of Evangelicalism derived more from Calvin in its dark and cheerless gloom than from the relatively mild Clapham variety known as Arminianism. Poor Ruskin, an only child, was largely denied playthings and playmates. Princess Victoria, to all intents and purposes another only child, fared better, although the distinction of her rank precluded her from free intercourse with other children. Nevertheless, she had one regular companion to summon to play: Victoire Conroy, the daughter of the Comptroller of her mother's household. Together they played billiards, battledore and shuttlecock, ball games, ran races, played with dolls, made paper dolls and, most importantly, blew bubbles which was pure fun — the very essence of play.

Ideally everything that children do should be sport and play, wrote Locke, and many toys and games were designed to help children to learn their numbers, letters and increase their general knowledge. Some of the toys in the early nineteenth century which the Drummond children might have enjoyed were decorative and ingenious. There were games

Untitled.
One of the youngest members of the family happily flourishing a bat. Though the name Alberich appears to have been crossed through it is quite possibly a drawing of him, in spite of his girlish appearance. Boys and girls were dressed alike sometimes up to the age of five or six. Alberic, Lady Gwydyr's son, was born in 1821. His dark green dress is another example of the heavy materials in which young children's clothes were beginning to be made.

57

Untitled.
Young children having fun playing Blind Man's Buff. More famous than almost any other children's game, it has been known since the 16th century by various names such as hoodwinke or hoodman blind, blindmanbuf, blinde-man buffe, and by Hamlet as hob-man blinde.

like the Polyrama, or endless changes of landscape, which consisted of a number of hand-coloured etchings each illustrating different features of landscape, to be put together in endless permutations. There were similar cards illustrated with letters, or animals, for making words or learning the species. Some of the most popular games were those which relied on chance, reflecting the love of gambling which in the 1820s was still thriving in the fashionable world to the dismay of the reformers. "A taste for gaming, as in men, arises from a want of better occupation," denounced Maria Edgeworth. However, Locke had realised the potential of chance as an inducement to learning and advocated the use of a dice with letters for inventing games to help children learn their alphabet. "So that," he said, "learning should seem a *sport* to them." Many of the chance games of the period had the dice replaced with a teetotum less associated with gaming than dice. At the same time they masqueraded as moral games under titles such as "The New Game of Virtue Rewarded and Vice Punished for the Amusement of Youth and Both Sexes", or "The New Moral Game of Merit" and so on. There were also puzzles like the curiously named "Dissected Puzzle of Correction and Finishing with Virtue." The accompanying book of rules states that "it is designed with a view to promoting progressive improvement of the juvenile mind". One wonders how seriously such assertions were taken, or meant to be taken. The most popular of all games of chance was "Pope Joan", a traditional straightforward gambling game. It was virtually re-invented in the nineteenth century and Frances Power Cobbe recalls that the severest punishment she ever received from her mother was not to be allowed to play "Pope Joan".

Some other toys of the period were tops, dolls, Dutch dolls, building bricks, dolls' houses, rocking horses (which were thought to help a child find its seat when put on a living horse), slates, pencils, paper, dissected maps, Chinese panels or tangrams (thought very useful in exercising the memory), backgammon and draughts (which relied more on skill than chance), and, of course, any number of card games. For physical exercise there were hoops, dumbbells, bats and balls, ninepins, skating, skipping, battledore and shuttlecock, and horse riding. In some areas hunting was so popular that a future Duke of Beaufort would not, it was said, allow his children to go fox-hunting more than three days a week until they were five years old. The 1820s were the golden era of the stagecoach and it became fashionable amongst the aristocracy and gentry to drive their own teams — sometimes they drove the stagecoaches. In fact, a further lament of the dancing master was that the graces of the jockeys and the coachman had replaced those of the dancing lessons.

The great object with children was to keep them occupied at all times: "Idleness in children, as in men, is the root of all evil," said Maria Edgeworth. Less severe was Locke's own observation that "in any case children generally hate being idle." To occupy them there flourished a welter of handicrafts and hobbies: Young girls, especially, embroidered, painted, cut-out, copied, collected, and stuffed all manner of objects — and all in the name of industry. In this category were the "generation of red and blue leather gilt-back albums with little flower-bordered ovals of crimson drawing paper" in which, wrote Sir Henry

A Garden Scene.
Strolling through pleasure gardens was a leisurely pursuit in which the young children joined the adults.
Stamped Cecil, August 1st 1828. Watercolour 7″ × 8″.

Durand to Cecily Drummond, "was an amalgam of bad prose, worse poetry, execrable prints, and eye-wounding daubs." More encouraging were the albums or collections of autographs, a hobby of equal interest and pursued by young and old alike. Particularly popular with parents because it "imparts instructive lessons and an agreeable occupation", it had become, in fact, "an affair of general interest", no doubt encouraged by the pecuniary value of a good collection. Princess Victoria was an avid collector, largely furnished with the signatures of the Great, by her uncle Leopold the King of the Belgians. To these could be added any number of other improving hobbies to wile away the long evenings, sometimes accompanied by a parent or governess reading aloud. Though there were few Daisy Ashfords, many children wrote imaginative tales in their leisure hours.

Princess Victoria wrote numbers of stories, one of which — *Sophia and Adolphus* — she claimed was in the style of Maria Edgeworth's *Harry and Lucy*. Another was a heart-rending account of a small girl who was packed off to boarding school to get out of her wicked step-mother's way. Emily Shore, a young diarist of the period, was more ambitious and by eleven years old had written a *History of the Jews*. When scarcely older she began an epic poem about Wittekind the Saxon, intended to be a work of several volumes of which she completed three. She also wrote a poem in the manner of Scott called *Don Roderick* and finished three cantos, as well as several other works. She died when barely twenty, otherwise she would surely have joined the league of the hugely prolific women writers who abounded in the nineteenth century. In the same category as these writings, though less ambitious, are those of Fanny Drummond, many of which have served as a source for this book. Apart from her long discourse, *Practical Education*, she wrote a number of letters in verse to family and friends, celebrating birthdays and similar events. She wrote poems of praise, and others about the pleasures and pains of her childhood. She praised her home Denham Fishery in an ode beginning:

Sweet spot! If now the muse were gracious
And gazed on me with looks auspicious
I'd cherish the deceitful hope
To praise thy charms as well as Pope.

She recalled her "oftshed tears" when young in a poem of farewell to her childhood, and she celebrated the pleasures of boating with her Drummond cousins in the following ditty:

Oftimes when up the Colne we go
To make some pretty sketches,
Our cousins cheer us as we go,
By singing merry catches.

Such were the pleasures which alleviated the trials of childhood.

FASHIONABLE ATTIRE

As HAS BEEN noted, most areas of life were of concern to moralists and religious reformers in their efforts to counteract the immorality which the example of George IV, both as Regent and King, encouraged. Fashion in dress was to prove no exception, and the figure-hugging fashions of feminine dress in the early nineteenth century were ripe for their reforming zeal, especially for that of the Evangelicals. One of the traits of the Puritan mind was a fear of the body: fear of its functions, of sex and of its naked presence. Therefore, the scanty and revealing dresses of the classical styles of the early 1800s predictably provoked their ire and indignation. As expected this was expressed by Hannah More, amongst others, in her *Strictures on the Modern System of Education*. She believed the introduction of these styles to have been the direct consequence of over-cultivation of the arts which, she had warned, "excite the imagination [which] becomes the most dangerous stimulant of the passions." She asked if one could not "rank among the present corrupt consequences of this unbounded cultivation, the *unchaste* costume, the impure style of dress, and that indelicate statue-like exhibition of the female figure, which by its artfully disposed folds, its seemingly wet drapery, so defines the form as to prevent covering itself from becoming a veil?" This licentious mode, she added, has taught us "to strip chastity itself of modesty". Indeed, the seemingly wet drapery was often actually wet, for dresses were worn dampened to make the wearer more statue-like. No doubt the rebukes of moralists were a force in the gradual shift away from these scant and simple dresses. They succeeded in implanting the idea of modesty in day wear but, despite their being joined by Queen Adelaide who, Greville wrote, was "a prude and will not let her ladies come to her parties décolletée", adding, "George IVth would not let them come covered," deep décolletée for evening wear persisted and became a convention right through to the 1860s. Perhaps prurience, like beauty, is only in the eye of the beholder. With the disappearance of the flowing dresses of the first two decades of the century went freedom, and feminine fashions once more reverted to constriction. The almost total lack of undergarments, a feature of these early dresses, was replaced by laced stays, layers of petticoats and bustles and pads, the foundations of the new elaborate dresses. Fashion had now taken for its image that of the sixteenth century,

Detail from At Breakfast, Easter Sunday.
Here a Mother and daughter wearing their new Easter hats gaze out of the window, whilst father reads the paper. The little girl in her leghorn straw wears it, one supposes, in readiness for church.
Signed C.E.D. April 19 1829.

made popular by the romance of *Kenilworth* published in 1821. To the tragedy of Amy Robsart, fashion added that of Mary, Queen of Scots and romantic nostalgia burst out in huge sleeves *à la Marie*, balanced by a billowing skirt, a small pointed waist and all crowned by an enormous hat. The effect was said to have been picturesque rather than statuesque. To these basic features were added a multitude of frills and flounces, *rouleaux and noeuds*, ribbons and bows, feathers and flowers, and trimmings of every description. Parading in exuberant colours, such as crimson, amber, ethereal blue, pink, grass-green, pineapple-yellow, *ponceau*, violet, yellow and rose, fashionable ladies like the Drummonds and their friends added considerable gaiety to their surroundings, carefully caught here by the young artists. Dresses, like people, were categorised in a hierarchy of classes: there was undress, half-dress, and full-dress. Within these distinctions came costumes for morning, walking, promenading, carriage, afternoon, evening, concert, opera and balls. The complexities of dress for the leisured was such that "the time of a woman of fashion is so completely occupied between dressing for, and appearing at, the morning concert, and the evening balls, that she can hardly allow herself to eat, drink and sleep. As to the duties of wives, mothers, mistresses, of families and so forth, it is impossible that any woman above the rank of a bourgeoise can find time to think of them." Said of French ladies, it was equally applicable to their English counterparts and a reminder that since the restoration of peace, France had once more regained her position as leader of fashion, with Paris as its Mecca. The Polite World continued to interlace English with French phrases. English was far too prosaic to describe the subtleties of fashion. "Our language will not describe shades of any sort; so matter of fact! For example the favourite colours in Paris are *dos d'Araignée*, *Puce en Couché* and *arbre de Judée*." French, too, added a kind of mystery for some of the followers of fashion. It was used to describe the huge sleeves which dominated dresses at the time, each designated *en gigot*, *demi-gigot*, *à la Marie*, *en beret*, and *à l'Imbécile*. They were all very full at the shoulder and narrow at the wrist. The fullness of the *en gigot* sleeve narrowed gradually down the arm to become tight at the wrist; that of the *demi-gigot* was full until the elbow and then very tight to the wrist and often extended over the hand. *A la Marie* sleeves were full all the way down to the wrist but the fullness was confined by bands at equal distances down the arm, and those *à l'Imbécile* were full all the way down to be gathered in a tight cuff at the wrist. Lastly, *en beret* sleeves for evening dresses were short, puffed and very full, imitating the shape of a beret which was often worn with them. The lady on p. 72 holding the hand of a small girl, is clearly wearing sleeves *à la Marie* on her outdoor pelisse. Whereas the lady seated on p. 67, in her white muslin morning-dress — undress — seems to have sleeves *en gigot*. Sleeves *en beret* are worn by the girl with a bared back, in the party scene. Another version of these sleeves is worn by the girl on the right. Inexpert though the drawing is it shows a short puffed sleeve covered by another longer and transparent one — a very popular form of this sleeve. Sleeves billowed on young and old, on undress, half-dress and full-dress and reached their climax in the 1830s.

Almost competing in importance with these large sleeves was the variety of headdresses

In a Brown Study.
This lady who is holding a book, very faintly drawn, wears her morning cap placed fashionably on the back of her head. Its blue untied strings or mentonnières *match the* Vandyke *points on her* pelerine *and skirt. May 1827.*

which completed the outfit. Forming an integral part of the whole ensemble were enormous hats, caps, bonnets, berets, turbans or toques each with a distinctive role. For morning wear, or undress and half-dress, there was a diversity of large, blond, silk lace caps, intricately intertwined with coloured ribbons and bows. Many of the pictures here have ladies wearing these caps and p. 66 is a delicious example, though crudely drawn. The blue trimmings on the cap echo the *Vandyke* trimming of her double collar, *mancherons*, and skirt. Elegant small blond caps, decorated with flowers, even made their appearance at the opera and theatre. This was partly out of deference to the other members of the audience and partly because the usual hat or beret had become too wide to force its entrance through the box door. For outdoor wear came a hierarchy of bonnets. There were rather plain leghorn or straw bonnets for walking, silk ones for promenading and those of the 'capote' shape, which were considered elegant enough to take their place in the carriage alongside the hat. These carriage hats with their enormous brims were ornamented with an esprit of feathers — a mark of the carriage hat, for feathers were "never seen on the walking costume of any lady who has any claim to elegance". Such hats with their elaboration of trimmings were worn over small, lace caps, and accompanied evening, opera and dinner dresses as well as all the other categories of full, or half-dress — a splendid example is the lady in yellow in the charade game. Hats shared their popularity with a profusion of toques, turbans, berets, and headdresses of hair — *coiffures en cheveux* — in which were mingled a fantastic blend of jewels, feathers and bows, carefully entwined through the large corkscrew curls of their wearers. "All the pride and pomp of aristocracy disappeared in the childish *embarras* of these ladies loaded — not adorned — with diamonds and fine clothes," observed that caustic commentator on English Society — Prince Pückler-Muskau.

Alas, children and young people's clothing was fast emulating the foolishness of their parents', marking the end of the short-lived golden era in their dress. From Tudor times until the latter part of the eighteenth century children's clothes had replicated adults, including all their inappropriateness — such as stays and petticoats, rich materials and confining garments. Thanks to the work first of Komensky, a Moravian, who influenced Locke, and then of Locke himself and finally Rousseau, all of whom fought for children's rights, childhood had become more valued and so had the idea of dressing children appropriately for that stage. The first recorded outfit specifically styled for a child, based on the criteria of comfort and convenience, was in 1770, signalling a revolution in children's clothing. The style reflected the Romanticism and back to nature call of Rousseau by borrowing from those styles worn by countrymen and labourers. Boys wore loose ankle-length trousers with soft lawn or cotton shirts buttoned onto their trousers with or without a short jacket. Called a skeleton suit this fashion lasted thirty years or more and was the inspiration behind the trousers which became general wear for men after 1825. Girls' dress was also liberated but perhaps because even Rousseau was conditioned by the male prejudice of his day, they never enjoyed the same extent of comfort and convenience as boys. They wore simple white dresses in calico, cotton and muslin, extensions of their baby-

The lady here similarly attired to the one on the facing page, though with red trimmings on her large white muslin cap, dress and buckled belt.

Detail from Interior scene at Scotsbridge, p. 19.
The lady is protecting herself from the heat of the fire
with a pleated fan which, most likely, folded. She is
wearing a large carriage hat decorated with osprey
feathers over her blond cap. At her neck she has a
double ruff. The same small girl who has appeared in
several of the drawings is at her side.
Signed C.E.D. 1830, Scotsbridge.

wear, right through childhood to adulthood, and by 1800 this fashion became that of the adults — the fashion to which Hannah More so objected. Dresses for girls were long like women's but to give them more freedom their skirts rose to calf-length. Unfortunately the rising tide of prudery in the name of modesty decreed that legs must be covered beneath the skirts, and so trousers, or pantaloons, were devised as more decent than petticoats. At first these were the same length as skirts but gradually they lengthened until the entire legs were covered. Women also took to wearing various types of bifurcated undergarments which eventually gave rise to the universal habit of drawers — a definite undergarment whereas pantaloons were not. Sensibilities were so delicate, and the desire to portray women as sexless, scarcely existing below the navel, meant that in early advertisements for them they were shown folded with the bifurcation concealed. By 1829 even the baring of young children's arms was reprehended as "a preposterous and unsightly fashion." One can only conclude that such prudish reservations over innocent things discloses how obsessed with sexual matters these objectors really were. It was the same misplaced delicacy which called for euphemisms like "interesting condition" for pregnant, and "inexpressibles" instead of breeches. As one contemporary put it, "A woman in good society sometimes leaves her husband and children and runs off with her lover but is always too decorous to endure the sound of breeches." Fear among the *nouveaux riches* of being thought vulgar also generated many of these so-called "genteelisms".

The simple white dresses, worn by mothers and daughters of all classes at the beginning of

A Scene in the Morning Room.
The children are dressed in their bonnets and caps ready for a walk in the spring sunshine, which is already
being enjoyed by the lady with a parasol. She is wearing a long veil to screen her from the sun.
Signed, C.E.D. Tuesday April 28, 1829. Watercolour $7\frac{5}{10}'' \times 9''$.

the century, underwent a considerable change by 1830. This was not just in response to the criticisms of the moralists, but also a wish of the newly rich to distinguish themselves from the rest of the crowd. Wearing their wealth on their backs was one way. Simple morning dresses had to appear as expensive as possible and were transformed by adding elaborate trimmings of lace and embroidered flounces of passementerie. In the same way children's white dresses changed, becoming big sleeved, whether short or long; full and stiff-skirted; tightly sashed and a vehicle for tucks, frills, embroideries and flounces. This remained a fashion for girls' party or formal wear for well over a century. It paid little attention to the vagaries of climate and many a girl shivered, as did Barbara Charlton and her sisters on their annual descent to the dining room at Christmas. The recognition that fashion could reveal class was taught to girls from an early age. At Frances Power Cobbe's boarding school, girls from fourteen years old had to appear *de rigeur* every day, which included wearing full evening attire of silk and muslin, gloves and kid slippers. They had to practise getting in and out of carriages in the appropriate dress, a wheel-less carriage being kept in the classroom for the purpose. Very young children also got caught up in their mothers' fashions, however absurd. The Reverend Gurney's daughter Harriet earned the nickname "mushroom" for staggering like the small girl here, under a huge hat which mimicked her mother's.

Boys, though faring better since their clothing was always more suitable, were also entering an era of restriction in their clothes. The demise of the skeleton suit was to put small boys back into dresses and petticoats with frilled pantaloons just like their sisters. Both boys' and girls' dresses became made of dark, stiff upholstery-type materials like the dress which Alberic, the small boy holding the bat, is wearing. For older boys stiff Eton collars were soon to replace the soft lawn ones of former days. Around the age of five boys exchanged their dresses for a high-buttoned short jacket with a frilly collar and ankle-length trousers as worn by some of the boys shown here. To these were added a peaked cap for outdoors and, in cold weather, a double-breasted frock coat called a "petersham". Sometimes the small jacket worn by boys was replaced with the newer fashion of a hip- or knee-length tunic belted and worn with a frilled collar and ankle-length trousers, such as the boy in blue, is wearing. In black, blue and brown they hinted at the sombreness which was to characterise male wear until the present day.

Perhaps the only lasting improvement in children's clothing at this time was the end of swaddling infants in tight bands, a custom which had prevailed since ancient times. Gradually decreasing throughout the eighteenth century, there are still accounts of the practice being continued in the first decades of the nineteenth century. By 1830 it seems to have died out and tiny infants were at last allowed to have their limbs free. Even so, the practice of wearing a belly-band for the first four to twelve months remained. It was thought, quite erroneously, to prevent ruptures caused by sneezing or crying. Some parents and nurses still persisted in the early nineteenth century in sewing up the bottoms of infants' sleeves and dresses ostensibly to prevent them from hurting themselves by scratching, but enlightened medical opinion was veering away from such restrictions. It seems that infants too suffered from many inconsistencies and contradictions like their older siblings, for they were often inadequately clothed in short-sleeved lawn dresses with low necks like the young infant here.

Whilst these changes were taking place in women's and children's clothing a quiet revolution had occurred in men's. No longer rivalling women in gaiety and splendour their dress had become a mere foil to feminine fashions. This was a legacy of Beau Brummel who declared that the dress of a gentleman must no longer be pictorial but must be distinguished by its "inconspicuous propriety". Discretion, it was hoped, would be a protection against the vulgar intrusions of the *nouveaux riches*. Within its parameters, though, there was as much scope for subtle intricacies in men's clothing as there was in its more flamboyant female counterpart. To be attired so that it could be said of one that "he always dressed as a gentleman" was the aspiration of most fashionable men, and this was no easy accomplishment for those not bred to it. As with women, there was a different mode of dressing for each activity or period of the day. A gentleman would breakfast in his chintz dressing gown with Turkish slippers; set out for his morning promenade in his discreetly-coloured frock coat; add boots and spurs for riding; change into his dress suit for dinner and round off the day in his ball dress or opera dress with his dancing pumps. He had the sleeves of his tail coat and frock coats made *en gigot*, which ladies copied, wore stays beneath to improve the fit of his close coats. He padded out his chest and shoulders with wadding, and his skirted coat in the 1830s swung out at the hips, also echoed by his female counterpart. An

Detail from The Cockfight, p. 54.
This shows a clean-shaven young man wearing a blue tailcoat, frilled shirt, light coloured trousers and black pumps. Very fashionable men had the sleeves of their coats made full at the shoulder, a fashion which since 1824 was copied and exaggerated by women — not the other way round.

Detail from A Scene in the Blue Room, p. 37.
Both the lady and the child are dressed for outdoors.
The child is as elaborately dressed as her mother, with
a tight waisted pelisse, sleeves en gigot *and a huge*
hat. Her appearance as a miniature adult is
complete.

Exquisite, or an Elegant or, in London, an Exclusive (other designations of the Dandy), required for wearing each week: "Twenty shirts, twenty-four pocket handkerchiefs, nine or ten pair of summer trowsers, thirty neck-handkerchiefs (unless he wears black ones), a dozen waistcoats and stockings *à discretion.*" He had, like his sons, renounced his breeches except for court or country wear and wore light-coloured pantaloons strapped under his instep, or straight trousers. A rich variety of waistcoats relieved the sombreness of his coat, and clean shirts with elegantly tied cravats were the signals of his undoubted gentility. To these basic garments, and the rules which governed the wearing of them, were added a hundred more to snare the unsuspecting parvenu: When to wear what, and what to wear with which and how to wear it; whether to leave this button undone or that, or have pockets with flaps or without, or to commit the solecism of appearing in a double-breasted coat in the evening, were the hurdles which society erected to confound those trying to join its ranks. The rules of dressing like those of manners would change subtly, just as the newcomer thought he had learnt them. "The English are the most aristocratic democrats in the world, always endeavouring to squeeze through the portals of rank and fashion, and then slamming the door in the face of the poor unfortunate devil who may happen to be behind."

Detail from An Interior Scene at Scotsbridge, p. 40.
This little girl in a characteristic pose of standing beside a seated lady, is about to take her leave for a walk. It is hard to imagine her being allowed to "run wild" when so demurely clothed.

FAMILY RETAINERS

IN THE SAME way that Society protected itself from the intrusions of unwelcome newcomers by erecting a web of defences in the form of rules and regulations, so it did against those who served it. Having devised a life-style wholly dependent on servants, it deliberately distanced itself from them, fearing the proximity which this dependence had created. For with dependence had come distrust. As the nineteenth century progressed servants were required to become as inconspicuous as possible so that their presence might not intrude upon the privacy of the family. This increasingly led to banishing them to attics and basements or separate wings from where they emerged via back stairs and baize doors when their services were demanded. These, and many other devices, such as arranging for their work to be done at hours which would not coincide with the family's presence, were resorted to in order to separate the two classes that dwelt under the same roof.

Distrust seems to have been an inherent condition of dependence in Society's dealings with its servants. Parents had long been warned of the undesirability of leaving children in their company. The still influential Locke had accused servants of inevitably undermining parental authority by acting as a refuge for children when they were in trouble with their parents, and so ingratiating themselves in children's affections — a circumstance they could not but use for their own advantage. He also warned of exposing children to servants' conversation, as their low-breeding and coarse language would corrupt children, teaching them evils which they might never need to learn. Though these fears in no way lessened during the intervening centuries, servants and especially nurses and nursery maids increasingly influenced children, a result of children spending more time in their company than in their parents'. Lord Melbourne said, in a conversation with Princess Victoria when she had become Queen, "Children learn everything from the nurse and servants", to which Queen Victoria replied rather reticently, "I'm sure, all I have learnt that was useful was from the nurse and nursery maid."

The tracts of unsolicited advice which, as we have seen, swamped literature on other subjects, poured forth about servants, addressed to both employer and servant alike. Maria Edgeworth devoted a whole essay in *Practical Education* on the perils of leaving

Mrs Emily Bunch.
Wearing a pink print gown, fashionable
ribbon-trimmed cap and demi gigot *sleeves, this*
pretty and youthful servant, perhaps a housekeeper as
her designation suggests, is almost indistinguishable
from her employer. Only her white embroidered apron
discloses her position as that of a servant.
signed Marian, aged 10.

children with servants, which, she hastened to add, were because of their lack of education rather than any inherent factor in their make-up. Her fears were endorsed by a mother writing from India, in a letter transcribed in Fanny Drummond's album, in which she prayed "that her children might never fall into the hands of servants". This very apprehension which families felt towards servants in relation to their children lent servants an irresistible fascination for the children. Crossing territories, if only into the kitchen to stir a pudding, could be an enthralling experience especially when coupled with snatches of servants' talk. Breathlessly committed to memory, these could be pondered over later in the dullness of the nursery, searching for secrets they might yield of this forbidden world. Trifles though these incidents appear, they could be major events in a cloistered life. Indeed, servants were for many children their only window on the world. Many a young son first perceived his manhood through menservants, and stole his first sexual pleasure from a young housemaid. One young member of the Drummond circle reversed roles and courted his Ashburnham cousin by disguising himself as a servant — a linkman — in order to have the chance to pursue his suit; this he did by pressing notes into her hand whilst handing her into her carriage.

As is well known, there was almost as much hierarchy below stairs as above; honorary titles like Mr and Mrs, prefixes such as upper and lower, and differences in dress served to distinguish rank amongst servants. Certain categories such as butlers and housekeepers, indisputably higher than others, enjoyed the privilege of better accommodation and being waited upon by their underlings. It was com-

Tim Toller, Coachy.
Wearing the livery of a coachman but minus the boots,
this burly figure in his breeches shows that these were
still worn by servants after their masters had gone over
to pantaloons and trousers.
signed Marian, aged 10.

mon for servants to arrogate to themselves the lustre of their master's rank, thereby raising their own status. A servant who served a peer would consider himself distinctly superior to one who served a gentleman. Children learnt much of the concept of rank through servants — watching their nurse stand up when their parents entered, and being prefixed by Master or Miss themselves, whilst they called servants by their first names. Servants were urged to accept their inferior station as having been placed in it by providence and therefore they should not desire to appear above it. They were continually exhorted to lead moral and pious lives, employers being advised, in barely veiled terms, that it was in their own interests to encourage this; for by aspiring to make their servants pious they might hope to prevent any show of discontent which servants' circumstances might warrant. Sanctioned by St Paul, one servants' guide took his actual words to the Ephesians, and likewise demanded absolute obedience of servant to master. Employers were told to allow their servants time to attend church regularly and according to one source were fined £10 for every month that a servant did not go. It thus became mandatory for servants and employers alike for servants to be moral. To conclude this advice, servants were told that their reward was the happiness which they brought their masters and mistresses. The expedience of moralists was endless.

However, servants did not always comply with the standards set for them and many employers were obsessed with their servant problem, a problem later encapsulated in Jane Welsh Carlyle who had thirty-four changes in thirty-two years and was only able to recommend one servant at the end. She never em-

Two children visiting a sick maid.
Two very small girls seem to have burst into this room only to have their advance gently checked. The quarters of servants, not least sick servants, were absolutely out of bounds.
signed C.E.D. June 27, 1827. Watercolour $5\frac{5}{8}''\times 7\frac{5}{18}''$.

ployed more than two at the same time and preferred to have only one for, as she wrote to Mrs Russell, "You can't understand the abstract disagreeableness of two, any two, London servants in one's kitchen."

The servants in the Drummond and Percy households are recorded here in the cut-out drawings, mainly the work of the two smallest Drummond girls, Susan-Caroline and Marian (aged eight). Their servants were clearly a source of interest to them in that they have drawn them with great care, especially the print gowns of the female servants. On the reverse of some of the figures nicknames have been inscribed, together with the nature of their service. Servants' appearances (even those required to be almost invisible) were nearly as important as their characters. Many must have found it difficult to hit the right note. If they appeared too well dressed they were accused of upstaging their employers, and if not well enough of letting them down. Their appearance signified the measure of the family's affluence. Generally speaking, lower-grade male servants wore their master's household livery. Like their masters they had dress and undress, their dress copying the fashion of a previous age. Countess Brownlow described the old-fashioned livery of the servants at Gloucester House in 1834. They were dressed "both male and female, as George III and Queen Charlotte, and wore straight frock coats with lace down the seams and black velvet caps on their heads". Collarless coats and waistcoats, worn with breeches, white stockings and black pumps, remained the common image for a footman for many a day. Their colourful and singular appearance reflected a desire to make servants ornamental as well as identifiable when on public display.

Edmund. A manservant and probably a footman, There is another sketch of a manservant called Mr Swift whom the children nicknamed "Nimble Dick".

a) *Nimble Dick.*

b) *Mrs —, nurse. There are drawings of two other nurses: one called Mrs Mifford, described as second nurse, and a Mrs Herbert, called Nursie.*
signed Susan-Caroline.

c) *A lady's maid. There are several sketches of ladies maids, all of whom are designated Mrs, thus suggesting that their names were those of their employers.*
signed Marian, aged 10.

The breeched and white stockinged burly figure on p. 77 was Tim Toller, the Drummonds' coachman, or Coachy to the children. In addition to his green coat he wore a red jerkin and breeches, also a part of his livery. To these he would have had a pair of boots, the signal of his work. On him lay the responsibility for the family's safety whilst travelling — sobriety then, as now, was his strongest recommendation. He also advised on the purchase of the horses, cared for the carriages, and, assisted by a groom, saw to the upkeep of the stables. As Lord Chesterfield sardonically remarked, coachmen were characterised by rheumatism, an inevitable complaint, whereas gentlemen suffered gout.

Though footmen were liveried servants it is possible that Nimble Dick, as his name suggests, was a footman despite not wearing the typical livery of one in the drawing here. Footmen were indispensable to families of rank, and fleetness of foot brought a distinct asset to a job in which running in front of the carriage had been a function. Though this was no longer required, an important part of a footman's work was to act as a kind of courier for the family. In a society where the demands of etiquette involved much sending and receiving of cards, their prompt and safe delivery was of prime importance. It fell to the footman to accomplish this by being quick and familiar with the geography of the neighbourhood or town. His outdoor duties also included attendance on the ladies of the family on walking expeditions, for shopping or visiting, keeping at a respectable distance, but close enough to signify his attendance on them in order to prevent intrusions from strangers. He had to sprint ahead on arrival at their destination, knock on the door for it to be opened by the time his ladies arrived so that they might not suffer the inconvenience of waiting. If the calls were to a relative he had to knock *and* ring the bell, a mark of respect, and a hint that some other members of the family had arrived; one of the nuances of etiquette which he had to learn.

Attending the carriage was also his province and the safe conduct of the passengers on reaching their destination was the footman's responsibility — no mean feat when the carriages were called after a ball. The chaos engendered by fifty or more carriages collecting together would make today's traffic jams appear trifling. Prince Pückler-Muskau described how some ladies were obliged, before leaving Almacks, to wait hours before the chaos was reduced to any order. "The coachmen on these occasions" he said, "behave like madmen, trying to force their way, and the English police does not trouble itself about such matters. As soon as these heroic chariot-drivers espy the least opening, they whip their horse as if horses and carriages were an iron wedge. The preservation of either seems totally disregarded." Injuries were a commonplace.

In large households, menservants' tasks were well defined, for the footman, groom, butler and valet had each their allotted duties, but in smaller families the footman and butler or footman and valet might be "united in one and the same person". It was prudent, therefore, for the footman to acquaint himself with almost every description of household employment — advice from a servants' guide of 1830. Personal attendance was generally a principal duty, but further tasks were the care and cleaning of lamps, glass, silver and furniture; the setting-out of the table; announcing

Mrs Wilson, lady's maid.
signed Susan-Caroline.

the guests, being well-versed in all the procedures of protocol, and attending the bells. In addition to this, the care of his master's wardrobe and dressing room might fall to him. In the opinion of the same guide, no position offered more opportunity for improvement than that of footman.

The principal manservant was the butler, except in very grand houses when there was a house steward. The butler's position was one of great trust and one which occasionally crossed the threshold into another social class; some butlers were actually received at tables of highly respected tradespeople. The butler's most important duty was the management of his master's wine and beer cellar, payment for these and for the coal. He was responsible for the arrangement of the tables, sideboard and side tables, and plate cleaning, assisted of course by the footman. He also waited on the drawing room. If the list sounds short its execution was complex. Dinners were especially elaborate with their great numbers of dishes and removes requiring orchestrating like complicated scene changes. The great wealth of the rich was rapidly turning domestic life into an intricacy of rituals which had never been seen before. After the butler came the valet, whose qualifications, as described by the enthusiastic author of the servant's guide, amounted almost to accomplishments. He had, of course, to understand the etiquette and fashions of the day, and his success in the latter sometimes led to it being said that "the valet cannot be distinguished from his master but by being better dressed" — an unforgivable error.

Heading the female servants was the housekeeper, the butler's opposite number. Mrs Fitzherbert see page 83 enjoyed that honorary designation which was a mark of the seniority of her years, itself a requirement for her position. Her responsibilities were the control of servants and the supplies. Female servants did not generally wear livery, those wearing it at Gloucester House being unusual. They were either too low in rank to be seen — their work being skilfully organised to be carried out when the family was elsewhere, or too high — as in former times when ladies' maids and housekeepers were drawn from the nobility. The black dress, organdie apron and cap, the symbols of the Victorian parlour maid, only came about when maids replaced the menservants and waited on the drawing room and dining room. The danger of emulating her employer in appearance was even more of a hazard for the female servant than for the male since at times she wore the cast-offs of her mistress. Generally, though, servants wore plainer and cheaper versions of their mistresses' clothes and were often the more attractive for it. The delightful printed cotton dresses with their fashionable large sleeves, which the young Drummonds have drawn with such obvious delight, bear witness to this. Only aprons signified their menial duties and even these were used to signal differences in status. White and delicately embroidered ones were more often worn by nurses and housekeepers proclaiming a remoteness from dirty tasks.

Ladies' maids, of which there are several here, accompanied their employers on their travels. They were responsible for the care of their mistresses' wardrobes and helping them to dress. Their knowledge and accomplishments had to be such that they could improve or conceal any inadequacies in their mistresses' looks. They had to know about reme-

Victorine Tweedle. A maidservant
There are several sketches of other female servants.
Amongst these are a Mrs Fitzherbert, housekeeper,
Caroline Octavia Collins, known by the name of
Quix, Mrs Buiff — Martha, uper (sic) housemaid,
Miss Litetia Collins, embroiderer and Anne Sharp
housemaid.
The average size of all sketches of servants is 4"×2".

dies for skin troubles, cosmetics, how to make pomades (ointments) for removing wrinkles, how to dye, curl and restore hair and how to remove superfluous hair. But in spite of the knowledge of the most intimate details of their mistresses, this did not give them a right to their confidences. Princess Victoria's governess, Baroness Lehzen, always read to the Princess while her hair was being arranged to prevent her talking in front of her maid.

There were other categories of maids: house, laundry, dairy and scullery — the handmaid of the cook who ruled the kitchen. Significantly the cook was paid a higher salary than the nurse or governess. In the Fox household, the cook received £10 per annum, whilst the nurse and governess received respectively £8 and £7. The nurse, whose status was akin to that of a housekeeper, was, unlike the governess, working class, but was distinguished from other servants by her unique task as a surrogate parent. Her responsibilities were to grow as parents distanced themselves from their children both in time and place, leaving the nurse to mould their children's characters into the shape which they had conceived for them. From these circumstances that unique English institution, the British nanny and her nursery kingdom, was to emerge to dominate upper-class childhood for over a century. There, in the remoteness of the nursery world, ruled over by their nurse, and fed on a diet of good and evil, stodgy food and parents' fleeting visits, children, like servants, were required to be quiet and mostly invisible. Like servants, too, they emerged at prescribed intervals. Liveried like them in their party clothes they made ornamental additions in their sorties to their parents' world. Belonging neither quite to this world nor to that of the servants, they lived their childhood out in the limbo of the nursery where they were prepared for the Victorian age.

EPILOGUE

IN 1787 WILBERFORCE set out to change the manners of society and so he did. This proselytising energy of Evangelicalism, together with that of moral educators like the Edgeworths, had succeeded in the task of raising a generation, which if not specifically Evangelical, was both religious and moral. Religion was the spirit of the age and continued so in the 50s and 60s. This was manifest in issues, amongst others, of church reform, or the Oxford Movement and the rise of Anglo-Catholicism. When Darwinism and science questioned the tenets of religious belief during the 70s and 80s, it was the dogmas not the ethics which were challenged. Even agnostics and atheists continued to subscribe to a Christian morality. Thus this generation (the Drummond children's) which had been steeped in the concepts of good and evil and the idea of parents, particularly fathers — however remote — as God's representatives on earth, found it natural to pursue the sanctity of domestic life with an almost religious zeal. It assumed absolute authority over its children and gradually, as religious observance became a convention rather than a passion, it changed sin into naughtiness, good and evil into right and wrong and disobedience into hurts against parental feelings. Though more secular than its parents it still imbued every small domestic detail with moral overtones.

Brought up on a host of moral tales when young, this generation developed from these a love of narrative which overflowed into reading and writing novels in quantities greater than ever before. Paradoxically, it was Evangelical writers like Mrs Sherwood, who, disapproving of novels themselves, must have helped create this love of narrative by the excellence of their own tales, a point made by Nancy Cutt again. As Mrs Cutt says, it seems more than likely that the Brontes, George Eliot and Charles Kingsley, all from Evangelical families, were brought up on such writers.

This generation also extended the reforming horizons of their parents, and their Christian consciences were manifest in the multitude of reforms which marked their era. They became solemn and respectable, and on a lighter note managed to give even the sensuous waltz a decorous image. The close hold became the barest touch.

The Drummond children grew up representative of their age. Fanny Drummond, whose own religious and moral rectitude had been amply evident through her writings, had a brother Heneage, who, not surprisingly entered the church. As already mentioned he married his cousin Cecily (Cecil-Elizabeth Drummond), the artist of many of the drawings. Their son Algernon served in India, where he achieved his immortality as the composer of the "Eton Boating Song", for which his cousin, Evelyn Woodhouse, wrote the accompaniment. Cecily's sister Agnes-Priscilla also married a clergyman, the Reverend Berdmore Compton. Susan-Caroline married yet another cousin, Harvey Drummond. Eleanor-Charlotte made the best match, as her father noted in his will, and married Vice Admiral George Woodhouse. Neither Julia-Frances nor Marian married, and history does not relate what happened to Emily-Susan. Mortimer, the only brother of these sisters, let the family down, not through his marriages (of which there were two), but through the debts he incurred all over London. According to one statement there were 63 outstanding debts in 1849 amounting to more than £3,000. These included Broadwoods, the pianoforte makers, Colnaghis, the printsellers, Fribourg, the tobacconist, Fortnum & Co, the grocers, and Hummel, the hosier. He had six different tailors, three hatters, three hosiers and three bootmakers and a perfumer where he spent large sums. Even in the best ordered society like that of early Victorian England there will always be those who cannot, or will not, conform to high moral standards and so provide a continual target for the zeal of the reformer.

NOTES

1. THE FAMILY AND THEIR CIRCLE

1. **p. 15** The children's father . . . Bolitho, H & Peel, D. *The Drummonds of Charing Cross* (George Allen & Unwin Ltd, London 1967).
2. **p. 15** Descended from an . . . Burke, John Esq. *History of the Peerage & Baronetage* (Henry Colburn Ltd, London 1889) p. 1050.
3. **p. 15** "prosperity . . . owes as much . . ." Note 1, *op. cit.* p. 110.
4. **p. 15** They were already allied . . . Unpublished History of the Drummond Family, in the possession of Mrs Barbara Fenton, a descendant of the Drummonds.
5. **p. 15** Intermarriages between these families . . . Note 1, *op. cit.*
6. **p. 15** many Drummonds being related . . . Note 4, *op. cit.*
7. **p. 15** Most were members . . . *La Belle Assemblée or Court and Fashionable Magazine* (George B Whittaker, London 1827). Terms used in this magazine and in the press generally.
8. **p. 15** Broadly speaking . . . *Survey of London* XXXIX. The Grosvenor Estate in Mayfair, Pt 1, "The London Season". 1841, p. 89–93.
9. **p. 17** Harder to gain entry . . . Beresford Chancellor, E. *Life in Regency Times* (B T Batsford, London 1927) p. 50.
10. **p. 17** "Take the hint . . ." *The Drummond Album* in the possession of Mrs Barbara Fenton.
11. **p. 17** It was satirised . . . Note 9, *op. cit.*
12. **p. 17** His flirtation with . . . *The Journal of Mrs Arbuthnot 1820–1832* (ed Francis Bamford & the Duke of Wellington: Vol I 1820–1825. Macmillan & Co, London 1950); quoting from Greville Vol II, 21st Nov 1833. p. 406.
13. **p. 18** "the most virtuous . . ." *Ibid*, July 1825, p. 406.
14. **p. 18** "associated . . . with all . . ." Note 7, *op. cit.* May 1830, "An illustrative Memoir of the Honourable Mrs Beresford Hope".
15. **p. 18** She and Lady Gwydyr . . . Note 12, *op. cit.* Vol 1, p. 385.
16. **p. 18** "even in the country . . ." *Elizabeth, Lady Holland, to her Son 1821–1845* (ed Earl of Ilchester: John Murray, London 1940) 7 Feb 1824, p. 26.
17. **p. 18** Her daughter Clementina . . . Burke, John Esq. *History of the Peerage and Baronetage and Knightage*, (ed Peter Townend 1970) p. 74.
18. **p. 20** It was alleged . . . Note 9, *op. cit.* p. 64.
19. **p. 20** Mortimer's sisters were . . . Burke, John Esq. *History of the Commoners of Great Britain and Ireland* (Henry Colburn, London 1838) Vol 3, p. 562.
20. **p. 20** It was a . . . Lathbury, R H. *The History of Denham* (privately printed, 1904) p. 390.
21. **p. 20** He also owned . . . Information taken from the will of Andrew Mortimer Drummond.
22. **p. 20** At Denham too . . . Note 20, *op. cit.* p. 207.
23. **p. 20** It is from a collection . . . Note 4, *op. cit.*
24. **p. 20** These cousins were . . . *Gentleman's Magazine* Vol 1, 3rd Series (London 1856) p. 782.
25. **p. 20** The "gallant" Admiral . . . Herts County Record Office. GH 553. Refers to Percy's acquisition, 5 Dec 1827.
26. **p. 20** He had one son . . . Note 17, *op. cit.*
27. **p. 20** "ruralizing", Lady Cowper . . . *The Letters of Lady Palmerston* (ed Tristram Lever: John Murray, London 1957) p. 37.
28. **p. 20** Additions and alterations . . . Girouard, M. *Life in The English Country House* (Yale University Press, New Haven and London 1978) Observations made in this book.
29. **p. 22** The small number . . . Trevelyan, G M. *English Social History* (Longman's Green & Co, London 1944).
30. **p. 22** This Evangelical movement . . . Henry Venn 1725–1797. His son John was rector of Holy Trinity, Clapham, the power-house of the Clapham Sect. He was one of the founders of the Church Missionary Society.
31. **p. 22** Concerned more with . . . Note 29, *op. cit.*
32. **p. 22** Evangelicals were instrumental . . . Rattray-Taylor, G. *The Angel-Makers* (Heinemann, London, Melbourne, Toronto 1958).
33. **p. 22** "The whole outlook . . ." Cutt, N. *Mrs Sherwood and her Books for Children* (University Press, Oxford 1974) p. 7.
34. **p. 22** "are much less addicted . . ." Aikin, L. *Memoirs, Miscellanies and Letters* (ed P H Le Breton: Longman & Co.) p. 304.
35. **p. 23** "Victoria is not to be fashionable . . ." R A,

M5/19. Duchess of Kent Memorandum, 7 February 1831.

36. **p. 23** to worship both Jesus and Mammon ... Tawney, R H. *Religion and the Rise of Capitalism* (John Murray, London 1926).

2. NURSERY YEARS

1. **p. 25** "the pleasures of the town" ... Rousseau, J J. *Emile*. Trans Barbara Foxley, (J M Dent, London & Toronto 1921) first published 1762, p. 11.
2. **p. 25** "pernicious stays and stiff jackets" ... Kitchener, Wm, M D. *The Art of Prolonging Life* (London 1828), quoting Dr Faustus in 1797 as saying stays prevented many mothers suckling their children.
3. **p. 25** These circumstances gave rise ... Wickes, I G. *A History of Infant Feeding* Pt. IV (publ in Archives of Disease in Childhood, BMA, London 1953) p. 418. The employment of the wet nurse slowly declined from then on until by 1900 she had become almost extinct.
4. **p. 25** In the 1820s ... Dewees, W P, MD. *A Treatise on the Physical and Medical Treatment of Children* (John Miller, London 1826, 8th ed 1842). Much of his advice is taken from William Cadogan's influential *Essay on the Nursing and Management of Children from birth to 3 years*, 1748.
5. **p. 25** It was feared ... Note 3, *op. cit.* Pt. III. Though wet nurses were said to be "mainly destitute of all reason, knowledge and principle" it did not prevent William Buchan in 1779 from recommending breast milk from whatever source.
6. **p. 25** Religious and moral pressure ... Note 4, *op. cit.*
7. **p. 25** Phrases telling them ... Rousseau in *Emile* also said it was a wife's "duty" p. 12.
8. **p. 25** "Of course Lady Arabella ..." Trollope, Anthony. *Dr Thorne* (John Lane, London 1902) Chapter 2 p. 40.
9. **p. 25** It seems also more likely ... Note 2, *op. cit.* p. 1267, quoting from the *Good Nurse* 12 Mo 1825, p. xvii. The "steel busk was worn in front of the corset, with the long stay, laced as tight as possible cannot fail of producing much mischief".
10. **p. 26** "Fashion decrees that ..." Note 4, *op. cit.*
11. **p. 26** These were urged ... Pinchbeck, I & Hewitt, M. *Children in English Society* Vol 1 (Routledge & Kegan Paul, London 1969) p. 349. These statistics are taken from Sir Kay Shuttleworth's *Four Periods of Education*, p. 121).
12. **p. 26** all five of Queen Anne's children ... Hopkinson, M R. *Anne of England* (Constable, London 1934).
13. **p. 26** Many untimely deaths ... Note 3, *op. cit.* Pt. III, 18th & 19th century writers.
14. **p. 26** "quieten infant's cries" ... Note 4, *op. cit.*
15. **p. 26** The laudanum bottle ... *Ibid.*
16. **p. 26** "continual crying" was so common ... quoted in *The Angel-Makers* from *A Letter on the Management and Education of Infant Children*, London 1827.
17. **p. 26** and hand-feeding ... Sterilisation of feeding bottles and boiling of milk and water as a result of the work of Pasteur and Koch did not become universal until after the end of the century.
18. **p. 26** These were still common ... Note 3, *op. cit.* Pt. V p. 501.
19. **p. 26** Treatments seemed hardly better ... Prescription book in the possession of Mr Denys Tweddell.
20. **p. 26** Master Percy was given ... *Ibid.* Prescription No 688, 1833.
21. **p. 26** His sister was prescribed ... *Ibid.* Prescription No 1302.
22. **p. 27** "Everybody, almost ..." Note 4, *op. cit.*
23. **p. 27** Nurseries tended to be ... *Life of Frances Power Cobbe by Herself.* 2 vols. Vol 1 (Richard Bentley & Son, London 1894) p. 32. The author was born in 1822. Mrs Beresford Hope (née Louisa Beresford) was her father's cousin. Her parents were Evangelical Christians of the Clapham variety — 5 archbishops as relations including Archbishop Beresford.
24. **p. 27** and near the attics ... Austen, Jane *Mansfield Park*. First published 1814.
25. **p. 27** The room doubled ... *Recollections of a Northumbrian Lady 1815–1866* (ed by her grandson: Jonathan Cape, London 1949) Barbara Charlton was related to the Duke of Northumberland through Sir Hugh Smithson. The family were Catholic. p. 28.
26. **p. 27** "too young to be my pupils ..." *Elizabeth Ham by Herself, 1783–1820* (ed Eric Gillet: Faber & Faber) p. 206.
27. **p. 27** Rousseau, and Jacques Guillemeau ... Guillemeau, born in 1550, wrote *The Nursing of Children*. He was a French obstetrician. Rousseau, in *Emile* p. 13.

28. **p. 29** "she can brook ..." Letter in the Northumberland Archives, Feb 1826, 29/26.
29. **p. 29** These, he predicted ... Note 27, *op. cit. Emile*, p. 13.
30. **p. 29** and the horrible Mrs Crabtree ... Sinclair, C. *Holiday House* (Ward Lock & Co, London n.d.). First published 1839.
31. **p. 29** "rod of iron" ... Airlie, Mabel Countess of. *In Whig Society 1775–1818.* (London 1921) p. 193.
32. **p. 29** "an unforgotten landmark ..." Note 25, *op. cit.*
33. **p. 29** Alas, instead of a place ... Note 4, *op. cit.*
34. **p. 29** "Twenty or more people ..." Note 23, *op. cit.* p. 46 Vol 1.
35. **p. 29** The aim of childhood ... Chapone, Mrs. *The Works of Mrs Chapone containing letters on the improvement of the Mind, addressed to a young Lady and Miscellanies in Prose and Verse.* 2 vols. Dublin 1775. Letter VIII "Politeness". There were over 20 editions of this work including the years 1821, 1822, 1827, 1829 and 1844.
36. **p. 31** Religious instruction formed ... *The Osborne Collection of Early Children's Books 1566–1910* Vol I (Toronto Public Library, 1958). A Catalogue. p. iv.
37. **p. 31** Her *History of the Robins* ... Trimmer, Mrs. *Fabulous Histories or The History of the Robins* (printed for N Hailes, Juvenile Library London, 13th ed 1821).
38. **p. 31** Her story of ... Sherwood, Mrs. *The Little Woodman and his Dog Caesar* (printed by and for F Houlston and Son, 12th ed. 1828).
39. **p. 31** Anne Jemima Clough ... Clough, B A. *A Memoir of Jemima Clough* by Her Niece (Edward Arnold, London 1897) p. 10.
40. **p. 31** Francis Power Cobbe ... Note 23, *op. cit.* p. 84.
41. **p. 31** "making religion repulsive ..." Aikin, L. *Memoirs*, p. 198.

3. THE SCHOOLROOM OR EDUCATION AT HOME

1. **p. 33** Hannah More ... More, H. *Strictures on the Modern System of Female Education.* The Works of Hannah More, Vol V. (T Cadell, London 1830) first published 1799. Like Mrs Chapone, her works were still reprinted.
2. **p. 33** "It clearly manifests ..." Quoted in *The Angel-Makers* p. 55.
3. **p. 33** The Evangelicals' aim ... Cutt, N. *Mrs Sherwood and her Books for Children* p. 10.
4. **p. 33** "religion should mingle ..." *The Drummond Album.*
5. **p. 33** "those talents and ..." Heberden, W M D. *A Dialogue After The Manner of Cicero's Philosophic Disquisitions* (London 1818) p. 68.
6. **p. 33** For girls, "born to submit ... *Ibid*, p. 70.
7. **p. 33** "domestic life is ..." Note 1, *op. cit.* p. 319.
8. **p. 35** Girls who, on reaching fifteen ... Gurney, The Reverend. Unpublished Memoir of his Daughter Harriet Gurney in the possession of Lady Harrod. The Rev. Gurney wrote of a "sort of finishing governess for Harriet".
9. **p. 35** "training in the Great Art ..." Cobbe, F P. *Life of* Vol 1 p. 60.
10. **p. 35** Despite the disapproval ... *The letters of Lord Chesterfield* (T Tegg, London 1827).
11. **p. 35** "to attain the best tone ..." Note 8, *op. cit.*
12. **p. 35** "virtue, should unquestionably ..." Note 1, *op. cit.* p. 60.
13. **p. 35** "Everything ... was taught ..." Note 9, *op. cit.* pp. 63–64.
14. **p. 35** "The pursuit of accomplishments ..." Note 4, *op. cit.*
15. **p. 35** Whilst girls were ... Note 5, *op. cit.* p. 95.
16. **p. 35** They were to be served ... Locke, J. *Some Thoughts concerning Education* (University Press, Cambridge 1880) p. 115 §134. First published 1693.
17. **p. 35** "The spirit of *caste* ..." Pückler-Muskau, Prince H L H von. *A Tour in Germany, Holland and England in the Years 1826–28* by a German Prince. (Effingham Wilson, London 1832) Vol IV p. 374.
18. **p. 35** Education therefore ... Note 16, *op. cit.* Locke said education of a child should fit his expected role in life.
19. **p. 36** "guided by the customary system ..." R A, M6. The Duchess of Northumberland on Princess Victoria's Course of Instruction, May 1832.
20. **p. 36** To inform the Duchess of Kent ... R A, M5/35. The lists were from Harriet A N Wynn, Henrietta Clive, Louisa Julia Percy and Lucy Herbert, all aged between 12 and 14 years old.
21. **p. 36** "women are seldom taught ..." Aikin, L. *Memoirs* p. 258.
22. **p. 38** She had to wait ... R A. Queen Victoria's Journal 9 Jan 1838.
23. **p. 38** Her children's books ... Note 19, *op. cit.*
24. **p. 38** "They inflame the passions ..." Chapone, Mrs. *The Works of.*

25. **p. 38** Maria Edgeworth disapproved . . . Edgeworth, Maria & R L. *Essays on Practical Education* 3 vols. (R Hunter, London 1822). First published 1798 Vol 2 p. 106.

26. **p. 38** Even the fashionable Walter Scott . . . Pelowski, A. *The World of Children's Literature* (R B Bowker & Co, London & New York 1968).

27. **p. 38** The Princess's week . . . R A, M5/33. Princess Victoria from her Mother, 24 May 1832.

28. **p. 38** "train of melancholy ideas" . . . Note 25, *op. cit.* Vol 3 p. 159.

29. **p. 38** "amusing without being trivial" . . . Note 19, *op. cit.*

30. **p. 38** "never be a day of gloom . . ." Note 19, *op. cit.*

31. **p. 38** "stamped this day . . ." Pückler-Muskau, H L H von. *A Tour in England, Ireland and France 1828–29* in 2 vols. (Effingham Wilson, London 1832) Vol II p. 10.

32. **p. 38** "the horror of Sunday . . ." Ruskin, J. *Praeterita* 3 vols. (George Allen, London 1886) p. 24 Vol 1.

33. **p. 41** "most enlarged view . . ." Anon *Advice to a Governess* (John Hatchard & Son, London 1827).

34. **p. 41** "sought a respectable asylum . . ." *Ibid*, p. 2.

35. **p. 41** "considered too low . . ." Charlton, B. *Recollections of a Northumbrian Lady* p. 31.

36. **p. 41** "life is a battle . . ." Note 33, *op. cit.* p. 19–20.

37. **p. 41** "The time must surely . . ." Martineau, H. *Health, Husbandry and Handicraft* (Bradbury & Evans, London 1861) p. 199.

4. PUNISHMENT AND CORRECTION

1. **p. 43** "is it not . . ." More, H. *Strictures* Vol 5, p. 44.

2. **p. 43** "make aware the knowledge . . ." *Ibid.*

3. **p. 43** "All children are . . ." Darton, F J Harvey. *Children's Books in England* (University Press, Cambridge 1958) p. 175, citing Mrs Sherwood in her book *The Fairchild Family*.

4. **p. 43** Obedience, that foundation stone . . ." Rousseau, J.J. *Emile* p. 53.

5. **p. 43** "Our natural parents . . ." *Mrs Sherwood and her Books for Children* citing *The Father's Eye* (1830) p. 48.

6. **p. 44** In the sixteenth . . . Schüking, L. *The Puritan Family* (Routledge & Kegan Paul, London 1969) p. 75, citing Batty's *The Christian Man's Closet*, 1581, p. 26.

7. **p. 44** "too often given . . ." Bamford, the Reverend R M. *Essays on the Discipline of Children particularly as Regards Their Education* (London 1822) p. 140.

8. **p. 44** "It (the rod) . . ." Anon. *Hints for the Improvement of Early Education and Nursery Discipline* (John, Hatchard & Son, London 1822) 6th ed. 1826, p. 41.

9. **p. 44** "if children are . . ." Edgeworth, Maria & R L. *Practical Education*, Vol 1, p. 378.

10. **p. 44** "The practice of setting examples . . ." Aikin, L. *Memoirs* p. 46

11. **p. 44** Obedience, too, for her . . . Note 9, *op. cit.* Vol 3 p. 163.

12. **p. 45** "to associate pleasure . . ." *Ibid*, Vol 3 p. 158.

13. **p. 45** "children giving pleasure . . ." *Ibid*, Vol 3 p. 169.

14. **p. 45** Both approaches . . . *The Drummond Album.*

15. **p. 46** Her behaviour did appear . . . R A. Princess Victoria's Conduct Books.

16. **p. 46** "Pretty good behaviour . . ." *Ibid.*

17. **p. 47** "Make me dutiful . . ." R A. Princess Victoria's Note Books.

18. **p. 47** "Let me show . . ." *Ibid*, 24 May 1826, A Morning Prayer.

19. **p. 47** "Dearest Mamma . . ." R A. 2117, 1 January 1829.

20. **p. 47** "Next to God . . ." Words taken from a sampler in the possession of Mrs Frances Felton dated 1812.

21. **p. 47** "Why should we always . . ." Essays by Abraham (1805–1819) and Charles (1806–1819) Elton in the possession of Lady Elton.

22. **p. 47** "incessant repetition . . ." Archer, R L. *Education in the Nineteenth Century* (University Press, Cambridge 1932) p. 98.

23. **p. 47** "The distinguishing mark . . ." Yates, G. *The Ball or a Glance at Almacks in 1829* (Henry Colburn, London) p. 6.

24. **p. 47** Mrs Sherwood described . . . *The Life and Times of Mrs Sherwood 1775–1851* (ed F J Harvey Darton: Wells Gardner & Co Ltd) p. 34.

25. **p. 48** "No sooner was a girl . . ." Wildeblood, J & Brinson, P. *The Polite World* (University Press, Oxford 1965) p. 223 citing The *Spectator* No 66 (Steele) 15 May 1711, Vol 1, quoted in *The Polite World.*

26. **p. 48** "nothing appears . . ." Locke, J. *Some Thoughts concerning Education* p. 42–43 66.67.

27. **p. 48** "never knew anybody . . ." *The Letters of Philip Dormer Stanhope, Earl of Chesterfield* (ed Lord Mahon: J B Lippincott Co, London, Philadelphia 1892) Vol 2 p. 165.

28. **p. 49** "at hand for the physical . . ." *A Tour in England, Ireland and France* Vol 2, p. 145.
29. **p. 49** "those whom nature . . ." *Ibid*, p. 145–146.
30. **p. 49** "a smaller waist . . ." Note 23, *op. cit.* p. 32.

5. LEISURE AND PLEASURE

1. **p. 51** "nature not only required . . ." Huizinga, J. *Homo Ludens* (Beacon paperback edition, 1955) p. 161.
2. **p. 51** "A girl who danced . . ." *Practical Education* Vol 2, p. 375.
3. **p. 51** The Quadrille was . . . Scholes, P. *The Oxford Companion to Music* (University Press, Oxford 1955) p. 853. Captain Gronow in his "Reminiscences" gives 1815 as the date.
4. **p. 51** First danced in Society . . . *The Times*, Tuesday July 16 1816.
5. **p. 51** Dancing with the . . . *The Angel-Makers* p. 91 quoting Burder in 1805: "Dancing of both sexes together . . . more or less must, I conceive, be liable to awaken improper passions".
6. **p. 53** "Even before . . ." More, H. *Strictures* Vol 5, p. 54.
7. **p. 53** Others, like the tract-makers . . . *Advice to Governesses* p. 100. The author said, "waltzing is so dangerous that I wonder how a prudent mother can tolerate the amusement".
8. **p. 53** "lewd grasp . . ." *The Poetical Works of Lord Byron* (William Nimmo, Edinburgh 1876) p. 103.
9. **p. 53** Mrs Sherwood . . . *The Life and Times of Mrs Sherwood* p. 15.
10. **p. 53** "held no dangers . . ." Carner, M. *The Waltz* (Max Parrish & Co Ltd, London 1948) p. 21.
11. **p. 53** "a frenzied gallop . . ." *The Ball or a Glance at Almacks* 1829.
12. **p. 53** But the seal . . . *Creevey's Life and Times* (ed John Gore: John Murray, London, 1934) May 20 1833, p. 365.
13. **p. 53** The term meant . . . *The Life and Letters of Cecilia Ridley* 1819–1845 (ed Viscountess Ridley: Rupert Hart Davies, London 1958). She not only danced all night and most nights, but she burnt the candle at both ends.
14. **p. 53** Until then . . . More, H. *Strictures* Vol 5, p. 64.
15. **p. 53** "Their invention . . ." *Ibid*, p. 64.
16. **p. 53** "The only natural feelings . . ." *A Tour in Germany, Holland and England* Vol IV p. 65.
17. **p. 53** "It really afflicted me . . ." *Ibid*, p. 65.

18. **p. 55** "supposed to increase . . ." *Practical Education* Vol 2, p. 375.
19. **p. 56** "To be present . . ." Note 16, *op. cit.* Vol 3, p. 361.
20. **p. 56** "Every mother who . . ." *Ibid*.
21. **p. 56** "combined with a . . ." *Ibid*.
22. **p. 56** "manfully or rather . . ." Panshanger Papers, Herts County Record Office. Lady Cowper to Frederick Lamb, n.d.
23. **p. 56** "for it helps us . . ." Forster, E. M. *Marianne Thornton 1797–1887* (Edward Arnold, London 1956) p. 59.
24. **p. 56** From the outpourings . . . Panshanger Papers.
25. **p. 56** to the puerile . . . Grossmith, G & W. *The Diary of a Nobody* (J M Dent, London 1891).
26. **p. 56** Hannah More actually . . . Note 23, *op. cit.* p. 58.
27. **p. 56** Other games popular . . . Opie, I & P. *Children's Games in Street and Playground* (Clarendon Press, Oxford 1969) p. 219.
28. **p. 57** As the Opies' . . . *Ibid*, p. 17.
29. **p. 57** "there can be . . ." Locke, J. *Some Thoughts concerning Education* p. 87 §108.
30. **p. 57** Poor Ruskin . . . Ruskin, J. *Praeterita* Vol 1.
31. **p. 57** Nevertheless, she had . . . R A. Princess Victoria's Journal. Compiled from entries for 1832.
32. **p. 57** Ideally everything that . . . Note 29, *op. cit.* p. 38 §63.
33. **p. 59** "A taste for gaming . . ." Note 18, *op. cit.* Vol 1, p. 5.
34. **p. 59** "So that," he said . . . Note 29, *op. cit.* p. 130, §148.
35. **p. 59** "it is designed . . ." All the toys and games mentioned are at the Museum of Childhood, Bethnal Green, London.
36. **p. 59** It was virtually re-invented . . . *The Life of Frances Power Cobbe* p. 40.
37. **p. 59** Some other toys . . . Toys listed and recreations recommended in the Treatise of Dr Dewee.
38. **p. 59** In some areas . . . Bovill, E W. *The England of Nimrod and Surtees 1815–1854* (University Press, Oxford 1959) p. 138.
39. **p. 59** In fact, a further lament . . . Note 11, *op. cit.* p. 6.
40. **p. 59** "Idleness in children . . ." Note 18, *op. cit.* Vol 1, p. 239.
41. **p. 59** "in any case . . ." Note 29, *op. cit.* p. 110 §129.
42. **p. 59** "generation of red and blue . . ." *The Drummond Album*. Letter to Cecil-Elizabeth

Drummond from Sir Henry Durand, 1834.

43. **p. 61** "imparts instructive lessons . . ." *Belle Assemblée*. An Essay on Autographs p. 212, 1827.
44. **p. 61** it had become . . . *Ibid*.
45. **p. 61** Princess Victoria was . . . R A Y61. Letters of King Leopold of the Belgians 1826–1835.
46. **p. 61** Princess Victoria wrote . . . R A. Princess Victoria's Note Books.
47. **p. 61** Emily Shore . . . *Journal of Emily Shore* (Kegan Paul Trench Trubner & Co Ltd, London 1891).
48. **p. 61** In the same category . . . *The Drummond Album*.

6. FASHIONABLE ATTIRE

1. **p. 63** She believed the . . . More, H. *Strictures* Vol 5, p. 58–59.
2. **p. 63** "a prude and will . . ." *Greville Memoirs 1814–1860* (ed Lytton Strachey, Roger Fulford: Macmillan & Co, London 1938) p. 105, Jan 19, 1831.
3. **p. 65** To the tragedy . . . Heroine of Walter Scott's novel *Kenilworth*.
4. **p. 65** Parading in exuberant . . . Fashionable colours from *La Belle Assemblée* 1827.
5. **p. 65** "the time of a woman . . ." *Ibid*, March 1830, p. 118.
6. **p. 65** "Our language will not describe . . ." *Ibid*, Jan 1827, p. 29.
7. **p. 65** It was used to describe . . . Details of sleeves compiled from *La Belle Assemblée* 1827 & 1830 and their details taken from Cunnington, P & Willett, C. *The Handbook of English Costume in the Nineteenth Century* (Faber & Faber, London 1966).
8. **p. 66** Elegant small blond caps . . . Note 4, *op. cit.* from the "Summary" of the first six months of fashion 1827, p. 321.
9. **p. 66** "never seen on . . ." *Ibid*, Jan 1827, p. 29.
10. **p. 67** "The pomp of aristocracy . . ." *A Tour in Germany, Holland And England* Vol 4, p. 351.
11. **p. 67** Alas, children and . . . Ewing, E. *History of Children's Costume* (B T Batsford, London 1959). Elizabeth Ewing describes the liberation of childrens' clothing as the "Golden Era". I have drawn on the book for much of the information on children's clothing.
12. **p. 67** Thanks to the work . . . *Ibid*, p. 42.
13. **p. 67** Boys wore loose . . . *Ibid*.
14. **p. 68** Sensibilities were so delicate . . .

Rattray-Taylor, G. *Sex in History*.
15. **p. 68** "a preposterous and . . ." Dewees, *A Treatise on the Physical and Medical Treatment of Children*.
16. **p. 68** "A woman in good society . . ." Note 10, *op. cit.* Vol 1, p. 21, 1832 Editor's note.
17. **p. 70** Simple morning dresses . . . Note 4, *op. cit.* August 1830, p. 73.
18. **p. 70** At Frances Power Cobbe's . . . *Life of Frances Power Cobbe* Vol 1, p. 62.
19. **p. 70** The Reverend Gurney's . . . Reverend Gurney's *Memoir of his Daughter*.
20. **p. 70** The demise of . . . Note 11, *op. cit.* p. 69.
21. **p. 70** For older boys . . . Note 4, *op. cit.* July 1830. A costume design for a small boy as described.
22. **p. 70** Perhaps the only lasting . . . Note 15, *op. cit.* The most influential work in which the practice of swaddling was criticised was William Cadogan's essay on the nursing and management of children, written in 1748.
23. **p. 70** Even so . . . *Ibid*.
24. **p. 71** "he always dressed . . ." Wildeblood, J. *Polite World* p. 239.
25. **p. 71** A gentleman would . . . Note 7, *op. cit. The Handbook of English Costume*.
26. **p. 72** "Twenty shirts . . ." Note 10, *op. cit.* Vol 4 p. 48.
27. **p. 72** To these basic garments . . . Note 7, *op. cit. The handbook of English Costume*.
28. **p. 72** "The English are . . ." Aywyos. *Hints on Etiquette and the Usages of Society with a Glance at Bad Habits* (Longman & Co.). First published 1834, third ed. 1836.

7. FAMILY RETAINERS

1. **p. 75** The still influential Locke . . . Locke, J. *Some Thoughts* p. 44–45 §§68–69, Locke really wanted parents to spend more time with their children.
2. **p. 75** "Children learn everything . . ." R A. Queen Victoria's Journal, Jan 22 1840.
3. **p. 75** The tracts of . . . Aikin, L. *Memoirs*. Lucy Aikin complained that tract-makers had dominated literature, 1834. p. 299.
4. **p. 76** "that her children . . ." *The Drummond Album*.
5. **p. 76** One young member . . . Information with the Drummond drawings at the Victoria & Albert Museum.
6. **p. 77** Servants were urged . . . *Ladies' Society for the*

Education and Employment of the Poor No 1 1805.

7. **p. 77** and therefore should not . . . *Advice to young Girls going out to Service*, 1820. A Pamphlet, p. 14.

8. **p. 77** They were continually exhorted . . . More, H. *Thoughts on the Importance of the Manners of The Great* 1830. Hannah More asked if it was not "impolitic" not to impress Christian principles on servants' consciences and that employers should encourage them to go to church. Vol 2, p. 136.

9. **p. 77** Sanctioned by St Paul . . . Note 7, *op. cit.* "Servants to be obedient to them that be your masters" Chapter 6 verse 5. Ephesians.

10. **p. 77** Employers were told . . . *The Servants Guide and Family Manual with New and Improved Receipts arranged and adapted to suit all classes of Servants.* London 1830 p. 252.

11. **p. 77** To conclude this advice . . . Adams, S & S. *The Complete Servant* (Knight & Lacey, London 1825).

12. **p. 79** "You can't understand . . ." Carlyle, J W. *New Letters and Memorials of Jane Welsh Carlyle* (ed Alexander Carlyle: John Lane, The Bodley Head, London, New York) Vol 2, p. 238. Letter to Mrs Russell, 20 Oct 1860.

13. **p. 79** "both male and female . . ." Brownlow, Emma Countess of. *The Eve of Victorianism: Recollections of the Years 1802–1832* (John Murray, London 1940) p. 162.

14. **p. 81** Attending the carriage . . . *The Footman's Guide.* 5th edition, London n.d.

15. **p. 81** "The coachmen on these occasions . . ." *A Tour in Germany, Holland, and England* Vol 4 p. 33, 1828.

16. **p. 81** In large households . . . Note 14, *op. cit.*

17. **p. 81** It was prudent . . . Note 10, *op. cit.*

18. **p. 82** The butler's position . . . *Ibid.*

19. **p. 82** "the valet cannot . . . Cunnington, P. *Costume of Household Servants* (A & C Black, 1974) quoted from "The World" IV 1756.

20. **p. 84** They had to know . . . Note 10, *op. cit.*

21. **p. 84** Princess Victoria's governess . . . Warner, M. *Queen Victoria's Sketchbook* (Macmillan & Co Ltd, London 1979) p. 12.

22. **p. 84** In the Fox household . . . *Two Homes* by a Grandson (Brendon & Son Ltd, Plymouth, for private circulation 1929).

8. EPILOGUE

1. **p. 85** In 1787 Wilberforce . . . Cutt, N. *Mrs Sherwood and her Books* citing Wilberforce: "God has set before me two great objects, the suppression of the slave trade, and the reformation of manners."

2. **p. 85** As Mrs Cutt says . . . *Ibid*, p. 75.

3. **p. 85** Cecily's sister . . . Unpublished History of the Drummond Family.

4. **p. 86** Eleanor-Charlotte made . . . Will of Andrew Mortimer Drummond.

5. **p. 86** He had six different tailors . . . *The Drummonds of Charing* Cross, p. 120.

INDEX

accomplishments, social, 35, 51, 55–6
Adelaide, Queen, 53, 63
Agar-Ellis, Lady Georgiana, 18
Aikin, Lucy, 22, 36, 44, 47
albums, 20, 59, 61
Almacks, 15, 17, 20, 47, 48, 49, 51, 53, 56, 81
Anne, Queen, 26
Arminianism, 57
Ashburnham, Earl and Countess of, 18
Austen, Jane
    Emma, 55
    Mansfield Park, 27
autograph albums/collections, 61

back-boards, wearing of, 47
balls, 53, 56
    Almacks, 17, 20
    baby or children's, 53, 55
beatings, 44
La Belle Assemblée, 18
belly-band, 70
Beverley, first Earl of, 15
Blind Man's Buff, 56, 57
boarding schools, 35, 70
bonnets, 66
breast-feeding, 25
Bronte, Charlotte, *Shirley*, 41
Brownlow, Countess, 79
Buller, Lady Agnes, 18
Brummel, Beau, 20, 71
butlers, 81, 82
Buxton, Fowell, 22

Byron, Lord, *The Waltz: an Apostrophic Hymn*, 53

caps, ladies', 66
card games, 59
Carlyle, Jane Welsh, 77, 79
chance, games of, 59
Chapone, Mrs, 29, 38
charades, 56
Charlton, Barbara, 27, 29, 41, 70
Chesterfield, Lord, 35, 48, 81
child-care manuals, 25
children's games, 56–7, 59
children's literature, 31, 36, 38
Christmas, 29, 56, 70
cinnamon-water, 26, 27
Clapham Sect, 22, 56, 57
Clare, Earl and Countess of, 18
Clough, Anne Jemima, 31
coachmen, 81
Cobbe, Frances Power, 27, 29, 31, 35, 56, 59, 70
cockfight, 56
coiffures en cheveux, 66–7
"Coming Out", 53
Compton, Mrs Agnes-Priscilla (*née* Drummond), 20, 85
Compton, Reverend Berdmore, 20, 85
Conduct Books, 46
Conroy, Victoire, 57
cooks, 84
corporal punishment, 44
country estates, 20
Cowper, Fanny, 29, 56
Cowper, Lady, 20, 56

Creevey, Thomas, 53
Cruikshank, George, 17
Cutt, Nancy, 22, 85

dancing, 47–8, 49, 51, 53, 55
dancing-masters (*maîtres de danse*), 47–8, 49, 59
decorum, female, 22–3
deportment, 47–8, 49
deprivation as form of punishment, 46
Devonshire House, 15
Dewees, Dr, 27
Disraeli, Benjamin, Earl of Beaconsfield, 17
drawers, 68
dress
    fashionable, 63–72
    servants', 79, 81, 83
Drummond, Agnes-Priscilla *see* Compton
Drummond, Algernon, 85
Drummond, Andrew Mortimer (father), 15, 20
Drummond of Stobhall, Baron, 18
Drummond, Cecil-Elizabeth (Cecily), 20, 59, 85
Drummond, Eleanor-Charlotte *see* Woodhouse
Drummond, Emily (*née* Percy: mother), 15
Drummond, Emily-Susan, 20, 86
Drummond, Fanny, 20, 33, 38, 41, 76, 85
    letters and poetry by, 61
    Practical Education by, 45–6, 61

Drummond, George, 20
Drummond, Harvey, 20, 86
Drummond, Heneage, 20, 85
Drummond, John, 20
Drummond, Julia-Frances, 20, 85
Drummond, Marian, 20, 79, 85
Drummond, Mortimer, 18, 20, 85
Drummond, Susan-Caroline, 20, 79, 85
Drummond-Burrell, Mrs, 15
Drummonds Bank of Charing Cross, 15
duelling games, 56
Durand, Sir Henry, 59

Easter, 56
Edgeworth, Maria, 38, 59, 85
  Harry and Lucy, 61
  Practical Education, 44–5, 75–6
education, 33–41, 44–5, 47
epigrams, 56
essay-writing, 47
"Eton Boating Song", 85
Evangelicals, Evangelicalism, 22–3, 25, 29, 31, 33, 36, 43, 44, 51, 53, 56, 57, 63, 84–85
exercises or callisthenics, 48–9

false books, 56
fancy dress parties, 56
fashionable attire, 63–72
  children's, 67–71
  headdresses, 66–7
  men's, 71–2
  sleeves, 65–6
  undergarments, 63, 68
  women's, 63–7
Father's Eye, 43
fencing, 48
finishing schools, 35
"The Fishery", Denham (Drummonds' home), 20, 61
footmen, 81–2
French phrases used in fashion, 65

gambling, 59
games, 56–7, 59
gastroenteritis, 26
gentility, "genteelisms", 47, 68
George IV, King, 55, 63

governesses, 38, 41, 84
Gray, Thomas, *Elegy*, 38
Grosvenor Place, Drummonds' town house at No. 6: 20
Guillemeau, Jacques, 27
Greville, Charles Cavendish Fulke, 63
Gurney, Harriet, 70
Gurney, Reverend, 35, 70
Gwydyr, Alberic, 18
Gwydyr, Clementina, 18
Gwydyr, Lady, 18
gymnastics, 48–9

Ham, Elizabeth, 27
Hamilton, Lady, 18
handicrafts and hobbies, 59, 61
Harrison, Sarah, sample of, 47
Hartford, Mrs, 47
Hawk, Mrs (Cowpers' nurse), 29
headdresses, 66–7
  of hair, 66–7
Holland, Lady, 18
Holland House, 15
Hope, Mrs Beresford, 18
Hope, Thomas, of Deepdene, 18
housekeepers, 82–3
hunting, 59

idleness, 59
infant feeding, 25–6
infant mortality, 26
iron chloride, tincture of, 26–7
iron collars, 47

Jersey, Lady, 17–18, 51, 53

Kenilworth, 65
Kent, Duchess of, 36, 46, 47
keyboard performances, 55–6
Komensky, Johann Amos, 67

ladies' maids, 83–4
Lamb, Lady Caroline, 56
laudanum bottle, 26
Lawrence, Sir Thomas, 18
Lehzen, Baroness, 84
Leopold, King of the Belgians, 61
The Life of Zwingli, 38
Locke, John, 33, 35, 45, 48, 57, 59, 67, 75

maidservants, 83–4
Maîtres de Danse, 48, 49
Martineau, Harriet, 41
medicines for children, 26–7
Melbourne, Lord, 75
Milton, John, *Paradise Lost*, 38
miscarriages, 26
More, Hannah, 22, 33, 35, 43, 51, 53, 56, 68
  Strictures on the Modern System of Education, 63
mother's role in child's upbringing, 25–6, 27, 29
musical accomplishments, 55–6

nanny, 84
neck-swings, 47
New Year balls, 56
Northumberland, Duchess of, 36, 38, 46–7
Northumberland, first Duke of, 15
novels and romances, 38, 85
nurses, 25–6, 27, 29, 84

obedience, 44

Paine, Mr, chemist of Rickmansworth, 26
Palmerston, Lord, 17, 56
pantaloons, 68, 70, 72
Percy family, 20, 26, 29
Percy, Lady Emily *see* Drummond
Percy, Louisa-Julia, 36
Percy, Vice-Admiral the Hon. Josceline, 20
Pestalozzi schools, 44
petersham, 70
physical correction, 47
physical exercise, 59
"Pope Joan" (chance game), 59
practical jokes, 56
public schools, 35
Pückler-Muskau, Prince, 35, 48–9, 53, 56, 67, 81
punishment and correction, 43–9
purgatives, 26

Quadrille, 51

religious and moral instruction, 29,

31, 33, 38
Religious Tract Society, 22
Ridley, Cecilia, 53
Rigby, Mrs (later Lady Eastlake), 18
Robinson Crusoe, 38
Roehampton, Drummond's estate at, 20
Rousseau, Jean-Jacques, 25, 27, 29, 38, 43, 45, 67
Ruskin, John, 57

samplers, 47
Scotsbridge, Percys' home at, 20
Scott, Sir Walter, 38
Selby, Lady, 18
servants, 75–84
    dress/livery, 79, 81, 83
    hierarchy, 76–7
Sherwood, Mrs, 22, 31, 43, 45, 47, 53, 85
    The Little Woodman and His Dog Caesar, 31
Shore, Emily, 61
Sinclair, Catherine, *Holiday House*, 29
skeleton suit, 67, 70
slanting boards, 47
sleeves, 65–6
    à l'Imbecile, 65

à la Marie, 65
demi-gigot, 65
en beret, 65
en gigot, 65
Society for the Suppression of Vice, 22
solitary confinement, 46
Spectator, 48
stagecoaches, 59
steel wine, 26–7
Steele, Sir Richard, 48
stocks (for feet), 47
Sunday Book, 38
swaddling clothes, 70

Tawney, Richard Henry, 23
Thackeray, William Makepeace, 17
theatricals, amateur, 56
Thomson, James, *The Seasons*, 38
Thornton, Henry, 56
The Times, 51
Toller, Tim ('Coachy'), 81
toys, 57, 59
Trimmer, Mrs
    Bible of, 38
    History of the Robins, 31
    prints of sacred and profane subjects, 31

Trollope, Anthony, 25

Udny, Mrs, 18

valets, 81, 82
Venn, Henry, *The Complete Duty of Man*, 22
Victoria, Princess (later Queen Victoria), 22–3, 53, 57, 75, 84
    autograph collection, 61
    Conduct Books, 46–7
    education, 36, 38
    gratitude to her mother, 47
    stories written by, 61
Villiers, Lady Emily, 18

Waltz, 51, 53
Westmeath, Earl and Countess of, 18
wet-nurses, 25–6, 27, 29
Wilberforce, William, 22, 33, 51, 84
Wilson, Thomas, 53
Woodhouse, Evelyn, 85
Woodhouse, Mrs Eleanor-Charlotte (*née* Drummond), 20, 85
Woodhouse, Vice-Admiral George, 85
writing stories, poetry, etc., 61